BUSINOMICS

MONEY TALK

From the Headlines to Your Bottom Line
—How to Profit in Any Economic Cycle

WILLIAM B. CONERLY, PH.D.

Economist, Conerly Consulting, L.L.C.;
Senior Fellow, the National Center for Policy Analysis

PLATINUM PRESS®

AVON, MASSACHUSETTS

TO MY WIFE, CHRISTINA, AND MY SONS, PETER AND TOM,
WHO ENDURED MY LONG HOURS OF FOCUS ON THE BOOK,
WHO SUPPORTED THE EFFORT, AND WHO CELEBRATED
WITH ME ITS EVENTUAL COMPLETION.

The Platinum Press® is a registered trademark of F+W Publications, Inc.

Published by
Adams Media, an F+W Publications Company
57 Littlefield Street, Avon, MA 02322 U.S.A.
www.adamsmedia.com

Printed in Canada
J I H G F E D C B A

Library of Congress Cataloging-in-Publication Data

Conerly, William B.
Businomics / William B. Conerly.
p. cm.
Includes index.
ISBN-13: 978-1-59869-119-1 (pbk.)
ISBN-10: 1-59869-119-8 (pbk.)
1. Managerial economics. 2. Strategic planning. 3. Business. I. Title.
HD30.22.C66 2007   658—dc22   2007000865

This publication is designed to provide accurate and authoritative information
with regard to the subject matter covered. It is sold with the understanding that
the publisher is not engaged in rendering legal, accounting, or other professional
advice. If legal advice or other expert assistance is required, the services of a
competent professional person should be sought.
    —From a *Declaration of Principles* jointly adopted by a Committee of the
American Bar Association and a Committee of Publishers and Associations

Many of the designations used by manufacturers and sellers to distinguish their
product are claimed as trademarks. Where those designations appear in this
book and Adams Media was aware of a trademark claim, the designations have
been printed with initial capital letters.

This book is available at quantity discounts for bulk purchases.
For information, please call 1-800-289-0963.

CONTENTS

ACKNOWLEDGMENTS

My friend and fellow economist Bob Whelan combines a head full of trivia with brilliant creativity. When my encyclopedia fails me, I give Bob a call. His contributions to this book were substantial, even though I didn't take all of his suggestions (and thus he and the others who assisted me are innocent of any errors that remain in the book).

Scott Conyers, Portland's ace investment manager, helped me unravel my own confused thinking in the chapter on the stock market. Peter Guyer used his years of experience in international trade to correct some errors in the first draft of the foreign economics chapter. Starr McMullen and Hans Radtke, two of my colleagues on Oregon's Governor's Council of Economic Advisors, gave the book a thorough reading and made numerous suggestions. My former research assistant, Rusty Fette, also made many very useful improvements in the book.

Early drafts of one chapter or another were read by Margaret Marcuson and Melissa Johnson, with each of them providing helpful comments. Dave Perry gave very valuable lessons from his experience in banking and corporate finance.

My wife Christina West gave me a good layman's response to the book, pointing out several sections that were unintelligible as originally written.

Tom Conerly III first put the bug in my bonnet to write a book. After half a century of sibling rivalry, the younger brother appreciates the older brother's confidence in him.

I want to thank my agent, Ed Knappman of New England Publishing Associates, for his confidence in this project, as well as my editor at Adams Media, Jill Alexander.

BUSINOMICS

Better Decisions Through Economics

WILLIAM B. CONERLY, PH.D.—In 1776, Adam Smith began his great book *The Wealth of Nations* with some observations from a visit to a pin factory. That may have been the last time that an economics professor actually visited a factory. My experience in over twenty-five years of applying economics to business problems has taught me that managers and owners need economics, but they need it from a business viewpoint. That is, they need *Businomics*. The goal of this book is to help business leaders make more profitable decisions through a better understanding of the economy.

Economics is not something different from business management; it is part and parcel of many everyday business decisions. Let's consider why economics is vital to business.

In 2001, bankruptcy filings by businesses totaled 40,000 cases, up from only 35,000 the year before. Corporate profits were $30 billion lower than in their 1998 peak. Companies were burdened with excess inventory and idle capacity.

Recession isn't the only problem that businesses have. In 2004, major steel producers were unable to provide product to all of their customers because of surging global demand for steel, primarily for construction. In 2005, tires were in short supply. Some purchasers of trucks and off-road mining equipment had to accept new trucks without tires—the dealers told them they could buy the truck, but tires weren't immediately available. These tire companies and the customers that depended on them should have been able to see the changes in world economics that were impacting them. The signs of impending shortages were there, but they were not incorporated into critical business decisions.

In a perfect world, businesses would be able to serve their customers' needs, with neither excess capacity and inventory, nor insufficient capacity and inventory. *Businomics* was written to help businesses create that perfect world.

If you love the pure theory of economics, in all of its mathematical elegance, this is not the book for you. This book is neither mathematical nor elegant.

However, if you think you need to know something about the economy to run your business, division, or department, then I definitely have something to say to you. If your to-do list includes decisions about staffing levels, inventories, capital expenditures, or financial structure, then this book has much to offer. If your "business" is a nonprofit organization or a government agency, you too will find *Businomics* immensely valuable. If you want to understand your investments in real estate or stocks or bonds, this book will help you there, too.

In this book, I've tried to make economics painless. *Businomics* targets people who have chosen not to become professional economists, but who also know that they need to understand how the economy affects their enterprise and their investments. I don't pretend that you'll find economics elegant, beautiful, or enthralling. Personally, I find economics to be all of these things. So do most of my colleagues in the profession, and that is why we became economists.

In a long career in business economics, I've met many businesspeople who have been exposed to the splendor of economics. Most of them liken economics to abstract art. They don't understand it, and they don't understand how anyone could find it beautiful. They nod their heads at the abstraction to pretend that they understand it, while they spend their time worrying about more immediate concerns like their sales targets in the southwest division.

Unlike my academic colleagues, I won't try to show the beauty of economics. Instead, I'll give you the tools to figure out why your organization did not hit its numbers in the southwest division, or in any other situation you may be faced with. I'll tell you how to learn to anticipate when your vendors will hit you with a cost increase. I'll advise you on how to look for new market opportunities. *In short, I'll explain how economics can help you run your business more profitably.* This book will help you to apply economics to your business, nonprofit, government organization, or to your investments.

Notice that I'm not promising to give you the answers themselves. The answers change from year to year. To know this year's answers, either hire an economist or read on and learn how to figure them out yourself. Once you learn how to figure out the answers, you can do a lot of your own economics on the fly, adjusting your operations as the economy unfolds. You don't have to like watching the economy for this book to be valuable; you just need to be interested in growing your profits. Even if you have economists on staff providing you with forecasts, *Businomics* will help you connect the dots between the economy and your business decisions.

Businomics is designed to make monitoring of the economy routine and easy so that you can spend most of your time serving customers' needs, confident that you have a system in place that will alert you to critical changes in the economic environment. After reading this book, your increased understanding of the economy will enable you to make better decisions, ones that will lead to greater success for you and your company.

BUSINOMICS

It's Not Just about Forecasting

WILLIAM B. CONERLY, PH.D.—Can anyone really forecast the economy? That's a good question. First, though, you should know the value of understanding economics even when it is not being used to provide a forecast. In fact, looking back at my career in economics, the most useful work I've ever done has been just explaining what has happened. For example, I spent some years preparing a monthly forecast of deposits for a bank. Sometimes the forecast was good, sometimes not so good. What was consistently good, however, was my explanation of what had just happened. That explanation actually helped the decision-makers.

Suppose deposit growth had slowed down. The executive in charge of the branch system would argue for paying higher interest rates. The CEO would glare back, suggesting with a stern look that if someone's troops didn't start trying harder, then someone would be out of a job. The marketing guy would want a bigger advertising budget, but the CFO would point out how many millions of dollars were already being spent with little measurable impact.

Now, let's hear from the economist! Sometimes deposit growth had slowed all across the country. Nothing we had done had caused it; it was just happening across the board. In that case, we would prudently decide to not start a price war over a general slowdown, not spend more advertising dollars over a misconception, and not fire the branch executive just because the Federal Reserve had slowed money supply growth. Instead, we would just sit tight and wait the situation out.

At other times, our deposit growth slowed while the market grew rapidly. This meant we were losing market share. Now it was time to look at the pricing and product mix. If we weren't competitive in pricing, spending more on advertising probably wouldn't solve the problem. But if our prices were competitive, then perhaps we had not explained the advantages of these products well enough.

Knowing how the economy affects a business helps in many ways other than sales analysis. *Businomics* provides the tools needed to understand a wide range of economic-business interactions.

For instance, economics can also help you understand cost increases. A local construction project in my city had an embarrassing cost overrun. At least, the first look was embarrassing. The project manager pointed out that steel and concrete prices had risen sharply in the past year, making the original estimate obsolete. At this point, understanding the problem required analysis of how large a contribution to the overrun came from excess steel and concrete costs. More importantly, the person responsible for the estimate should have been taken to task for not understanding the volatility of steel and concrete prices. Both prices fluctuate a great deal, as we'll discuss later, and a wise business leader considers the risk of cost increases before committing to a project at a fixed price.

Sometimes the economics even shows that we're *not* doing our jobs well. For example, if the market is growing, sales of similar products at your competitors are growing, and your pricing is in line with your competitors, then something is amiss if sales of your product are *not* growing. Your marketing people somehow aren't getting the job done, and it may be time for departmental restructuring. But it's better for heads to roll as a result of poor performance than because of a mistaken interpretation of the sales data.

Economics helps decision-makers even before they develop a forecast.

KEY POINT

Understanding economics can help you to diagnose the causes
of increases or decreases in sales volumes and costs.

CREATING FORECASTS AND MAKING DECISIONS

Decisions are about the future. We don't make decisions about the past or even about the present. Decisions are always about the future. Should we build new capacity *to serve future demand*? Should we lower our prices today *to boost sales between now and the end of the quarter*? Will it be cheaper *over the next five years* to have fixed-rate debt or floating-rate debt? Will George get his division profitable *next year* or should I bring in new management?

Decisions about the future must have a vision of what the future will look like. People who claim that nobody can forecast the future haven't really thought this through. If your home has a southern exposure, then you think that the path of the sun through the sky will continue along historical patterns. If you continue to produce whatever it is you have always produced, then you think demand for that product will continue. If you build only to order, you think that the price you could get selling goods off the shelf would not justify the risk that new orders will not come in. Whether you're optimistic or pessimistic, you have a view of the future.

> **"Whether you're optimistic or pessimistic, you have a view of the future."**

Some businesses try to get away from dependence on an economic forecast. They shorten product development cycles, and they use real-time supply-chain management and production techniques. Dell Computer has earned widespread respect in this regard. Does the economic forecaster like the trend? Actually, I think it's pretty cool. I know that forecasts aren't perfect, and I like to see businesses not be overly dependent on an economic forecast. But take note of all the economic assumptions about the future that are built into Dell's business model.

The first assumption is that the total volume of business will justify the infrastructure costs of the systems. This process entails far more complexity than simply buying a bunch of raw materials, assembling them, and selling the finished goods when orders are received. Such complexity costs money. Is the expense justified? Maybe, maybe not. A state-of-the-art buggy-whip business with real-time supply-chain management is still just a buggy-whip business.

The second economic assumption of the Dell model is that the variety of products desired by customers will be large and unpredictable. If, instead, consumers consistently prefer configuration A, then a company that only produces the one configuration will probably have lower costs than a company set up to offer a variety of options. Look at the car industry, where the Japanese gained tremendous market share partly by offering fewer options. They put the most popular features in the base model, offered a few different colors, and didn't bother setting up factories that could produce a wide variety of configurations. They built cars at a lower cost, and the buying experience was far more customer friendly.

A few years ago, two decades after the Japanese had implemented their approach, I went shopping for a new car. I confirmed that this trend continues. The Chrysler salesman thought I could buy the larger engine and extended wheelbase without tinted windows and certain other options, but he couldn't find a car configured that way on his lot. Maybe it's not available, he said. The Honda saleswoman showed me two models, one of which had a single option. Four colors. A total of twelve combinations. Simple. Take it or leave it. Guess which car I bought?

The electric power industry offers a good example of businesses trying to wean themselves from economic forecasts. After decades of building large plants, they have switched to smaller facilities. The experts on production costs will still grant that the large plants cost less to run per kilowatt-hour of electricity. But if the plant runs at less than full capacity while waiting for electricity demand to reach the forecasted level, then the cost becomes pretty high. The electricity industry now realizes that demand is hard to forecast. It cannot justify large capital expenditures that make sense only with a highly certain demand forecast. Instead, they build lots of small plants, giving themselves protection against bad forecasts, at the cost of higher average generating costs. But remember: This skepticism about forecasting is itself a forecast. It's a forecast about the volatility of demand, and about our ability to anticipate demand. That makes it a forecast about a forecast—but a forecast nonetheless.

Finally, let's talk about how we form a forecast, whether it's a forecast for the sales of a product, one about the volatility of sales, or one about the potential accuracy of a sales forecast. We don't have to rely on just economists to do the job; we could instead ask the marketing department, the engineering department, or a good seasoned manager.

My experience suggests that marketing people see current trends pretty well, but they don't anticipate changes in these trends nearly as well as economists do. Coming out of the 1991–92 recession, the bank where I was working had commercial loan volume that stunk. The economy picked up, but commercial loan volume continued to be low. The marketing people were focused on our sales techniques and our position within the market. I was nervous that a few good people would be fired. Looking at past recessions, it was clear to me that commercial loan volumes were always low for a year or two after the end of the recession. At some point, though, volume always came back. And when that volume came back, it didn't just creep up, it shot up like a rocket. That was the historical pattern, which I explained to the bankers.

Fortunately, I was convincing enough that the bank didn't lay off staff while we waited for the upturn. When the upturn came, we had a seasoned management team still in place, with plenty of loan officers and credit administrators still at work to meet the demand.

Engineers make forecasts, but they often tend to look for fixed relationships. Engineers used to make forecasts in the electric utility industry. In the late 1970s, a team at Pacific Gas & Electric Company anticipated continued strong demand for electricity, sufficient to justify building a $1 billion coal-fired power plant, in addition to the billion-dollar nuclear plant then in development. Economists took a stab at the forecast, and came up with much lower numbers. They had put some price effects into their model—because prices were higher, then demand would be lower than one would otherwise expect. The engineers didn't see any immediate price effects, but the economists said that they take time to develop. Company management bought the economists' forecast and scrubbed the coal-fired plant from the corporate plans. Who was right? Looking back, both forecasts were pretty far off the mark. But the economists' forecast was closer to the truth, and the new plant was clearly not needed in the 1980s and most of the 1990s. The team of economists saved the organization a billion dollars.

> **"A good manager's judgment can often provide an accurate forecast, although it may be constrained by the limits of the manager's experience."**

A good manager's judgment can often provide an accurate forecast, although it may be constrained by the limits of the manager's experience. As a young bank economist, I developed a quantitative model of the seasonal pattern of our deposits. I found that there was an experienced manager at the bank who had figured out the seasonal pattern without a bit of statistical theory. After thirty years of watching the numbers, he knew them intuitively. It was more than a little disconcerting to me to see my slick scientific approach equaled by seat-of-the-pants judgment. A few years later, though, the story was different. We combined five banks that had been independent and operating in different states into one regional bank. The management team came from across the region, and its members had very different ideas of where our deposits were going. It turned out that there were some very different seasonal patterns across the states because of when state tax payments were made. The people who knew the Oregon pattern were misinterpreting Washington, and vice versa. Applied economics then came to the rescue, explaining why the seasoned judgment of good managers was now out of kilter.

There's a place for an economic approach to forecasting. No forecast is likely to be perfect, but fundamental relationships can help anyone form a more accurate view of the future. The forecasts used in business might be verbal rather than numerical. Adjectives are more common than decimal places. But every decision-maker has a vision of the future, whether that vision is expressed in numbers, words, or graphs. That vision can be enhanced with an understanding of economics.

Discussions of forecast accuracy can be too numerical. Let's say I predicted growth of gross domestic product (GDP) of 3.5 percent, but it actually came in at 3.2 percent. Was I wrong, or was I pretty much on target? In fact, neither a business manager nor a consumer can tell the difference between 3.2 percent and 3.5 percent growth. The economic difference is outweighed by differences to the business caused by its own managerial decisions. That's why I often provide forecasts in adjectives rather than in numbers. The economy can be described in the following ways:

- Very strong
- Strong
- Moderate
- Weak
- Very weak

The adjectives provide more value for most businesses than a numerical GDP forecast. The challenge for a business leader is anticipating changes in the adjectives. Knowing that economic growth will shift from "strong" to at least "moderate" and possibly "weak" is as much as a business leader really needs. With a good understanding of how the economy works, that degree of accuracy is readily possible.

KEY POINTS

Business decisions are about the future and must rely on a view of the future.	Economics can help you to form a more accurate vision of the future, compared to other common methods of forecasting.	As a business manager, you should focus more on the broad magnitudes of changes rather than on the specific numbers.

BUSINOMICS

MONEY TALK

Cycles in Your Sector of the Economy

WILLIAM B. CONERLY, PH.D.—What does a manager need to know about the economy? Let's back up and ask, instead, this question: What does a manager need to know about fluctuations in his or her business?

The manager would like to know when downturns—and upturns—in sales are coming. When the economy accelerates or slows down, the manager would like to know how deep a decline will be, or how steep the increase will be. How long will sales remain depressed, or how long will the boom last? Can we raise prices without losing too much in sales?

Sales are not dependent solely on the economy. The quality of a company's products, service, and marketing efforts play a major role. Nonetheless, the economy also plays a significant role in the level of sales that companies experience.

Managers would also like to know when their costs are going to rise or fall. The economy, again, causes some costs to rise or fall, though other factors are also at work. When fuel costs rise, for instance, the cause is often strong economic growth around the world. The future course of interest rates plays a key role in financial strategy at many companies. Some small businesses will go along merrily with little borrowing and with excess cash paid to the owner's personal checking account. Many other firms, however, have to borrow to meet their capital needs, making interest expense a critical cost. In this chapter, I'll present the economic information necessary for you as a manager to know the answers to these questions.

HISTORICAL EXPERIENCE

Let's begin by looking at the historical experience of the United States economy in the post-war era.

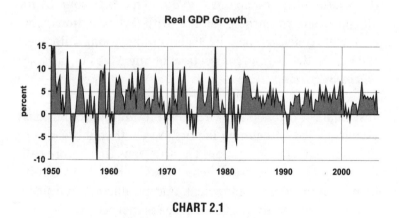

Real GDP Growth

CHART 2.1

The areas below the 0 percent line show declines in gross domestic product (GDP), which measures the overall economy. The data used in this graph are adjusted for inflation, so they represent actual quantities, rather than dollars worth of sales. Not every decline in GDP constitutes a recession, as we'll learn later, but recessions are always characterized by a drop in GDP. From a business manager's viewpoint, recessions have to be a major concern. Declines in economic growth of 1 or 2 percentage points are usually felt by businesses, but they don't threaten survival.

However, when the economy goes into recession, many businesses face major risks to their continued existence. That said, too much attention is paid to whether a business slowdown qualifies as a technical recession. News accounts will focus on the issue, and the politicians usually weigh in on the subject. In practical terms, however, a significant slowdown has meaning to businesses even if it does not qualify as an official recession. Nonetheless, looking at recessions helps business managers to understand the external winds that buffet their companies. (*Note:* The data sources for all charts shown in the book are, with few exceptions, government agencies. They are listed online, along with their URLs, in the Resources section of my Website, at *www.businomics.com.*)

Just what is a recession? It's a general contraction of business activity. The two defining factors are depth and breadth of the downturn in production. Depth means that before calling an episode a recession, economists want to see a significant drop in sales, employment, and production, not just a small, temporary drop. Breadth means that economists look for economic weakness to have spread through much of the economy. So your industry may go into a severe downturn, but if the weakness doesn't spread to the rest of the economy, we won't call it a recession.

▶ Gross domestic product (GDP) constitutes the market value of the goods and services produced within the United States. A slightly different concept, gross national product (GNP), served as the main gauge of economic production for many years.

Calculation of GDP begins with sales to final customers. The major categories are consumer spending, investment in physical equipment and facilities by business, residential construction, government purchases of goods and services, and net exports.

Intermediate transactions don't count. For instance, when I buy a bottle of beer, that counts as a part of GDP. But when the bottle manufacturer sold the empty bottle to the beer brewer, that was not part of GDP, because the bottle had not yet been sold to the final customer. If we had counted both transactions, we would be counting the value of the empty bottle twice.

Counting sales is the not same as counting production, however, so we add to sales any increase in inventories in the economy. The increase in inventories constitutes goods produced that were not sold. By adding it to sales, we have a measure of production.

Exports are counted as GDP, just as any other sale is counted. Imports, however, pose a problem. When we counted sales in the economy, we counted some goods that were not produced here. My beer, for example, might have been imported. So after counting all sales in the country, we subtract the total value of imports.

Finally, government spending is not entirely part of GDP. When the government buys goods and services, including the labor services of its employees, that counts as part of GDP. But when the government sends out a Social Security check, that does not count as GDP; rather, that is called a transfer payment.

"Real" GDP is economist jargon for "inflation-adjusted" GDP. We usually refer to this unless we explicitly say "nominal" GDP, which is an economist's term for data not adjusted for inflation.

TABLE 2-A. Post-War Recessions and Expansions

Beginning of recession	End of recession	Length of recession (months)	Length of following expansion (months)	Length of total cycle, peak-to-peak (months)
November 1948	October 1949	11	45	56
July 1953	May 1954	10	39	49
August 1957	April 1958	8	24	32
April 1960	February 1961	10	106	116
December 1969	November 1970	11	36	47
November 1973	March 1975	16	58	74
January 1980	July 1980	6	12	18
July 1981	November 1982	16	92	108
July 1990	March 1991	8	120	128
March 2001	November 2001	9	TBD*	TBD*

TBD: to be determined after the current expansion is over.

The length of recessions averages about eleven months, with a range from six to sixteen months. Since the earliest good data (1854), the longest recession lasted more than five years, from 1873 to 1879. The shortest recession on record is still the 1980 recession, though that was quickly followed by the 1981–1982 recession. Most economists think of those two recessions as a single event, which at the time was called the "double dip."

The label "business cycle" may be misleading, especially to anyone who thinks of cycles such as sine waves or ocean waves. Unlike cycles in physics, business cycles do not have regular periods (the length of time or distance from peak to peak). Nor are the magnitudes of changes from peak to trough consistent from one business cycle to another. You can find some regular patterns regarding the timing of different sectors relative to the overall economy, something we'll discuss later. There are also some regularities about which sectors have larger-than-average changes, and which have smaller-than-average changes. This information will be critical to business managers in their contingency planning.

Statistical analysis of the data on business cycles shows that the probability of a recession remains fairly steady through time. When an expansion has been running for many years, longer than the average expansion, pundits sometimes say that we are due for a recession. Others argue that in these cases, we have to work increasingly hard to fight the inexorable tendency toward recession. These assertions rely on a false interpretation of the data. Actually, the tendency to recession is just as strong one year into an expansion as ten years into an expansion.

BUSINOMICS JARGON MADE CLEAR: *RECESSION*

▶ The business press often uses the shorthand definition of a recession as being two consecutive quarters of declining real gross domestic product. The closest thing the United States has to an official definition is the decision by a private organization, the Business Cycle Dating Committee of the National Bureau of Economic Research. This committee of scholars looks at a number of the measures that capture the depth and breadth of a downturn.

Although the Dating Committee makes the final decision, you shouldn't look to them for help. First, they report on the past, rather than forecast the future. So they won't tell you when they think a recession is imminent. Second, the Business Cycle Dating Committee waits for a good deal of data to be available before determining dates. Thus, six or more months may lag between the turning point—such as when the economy went into recession—and the committee's announcement. By the time they make the call, everyone who's going to feel the recession's pain has already felt it. In fact, some sectors may already be starting to recover.

Recessions are akin to automobile accidents. No single recession *has* to happen. We can always point out the causes and sketch out how the downturn could have been avoided, through better monetary policy or other means. But like accidents, recessions happen. Mistakes will be made, at some point, which will reduce the economy's margin for error. Other mistakes or external shocks will push the economy over the edge, into recession. We may not know when, and we may try to avoid them, but recessions will happen from time to time.

Recessions have been milder and rarer in the last fifty years than in the preceding years of American history. Economists still debate the details, but here are the rough recessionary facts for half-century periods (beginning in 1854):

TABLE 2-B. Recessions

	1854–1900	1900–1950	1950–2000
Number of recessions	11	12	8
Total months of recession	237	217	85
Average length (months)	22	18	11

The number of recessions has certainly declined, but the average length of recession has dropped even more. Businesses today are fortunate not to face the high risk of recession of the pre–World War II era, not that anyone really has a choice about which century he or she does business in. However, even in recent years, recessions pose a genuine risk to business. On average, we have had a recession about once every six years, each one lasting just under one year. That has to give pause to anyone sketching out a five-year business plan.

The greater stability of the economy in recent years has a sound economic foundation. First, economic production has shifted away from goods toward services. Consumption of services tends to be more stable, as we discuss below. Second, inventory swings have been very destabilizing to the economy in the past. However, businesses have been reducing their average inventory levels, as well as monitoring changes in inventories more closely. The result of these business practices has been to soften inventory swings, which in turn has reduced the volatility of the entire economy.

These two issues, the rise of the service sector and the muting of inventory swings, actually interact, as services cannot be stored over time, so there is no inventory swing in the service sector.

Will the stabilizing trend continue? My guess is yes, meaning that future recessions will be milder and less frequent. However, the business cycle is not over. Businesses need to plan for the occasional downturn even though the economy will grow during most years.

At this point, let's summarize.

KEY POINTS		
Recessions happen occasionally, but not on any fixed schedule.	Recessions average just less than a year of duration, but they can be shorter or longer.	No particular recession is inevitable, but the occurrence of *some* recession at *some* time in the next ten or twenty years does seem inevitable.

PROFITS ACROSS THE ECONOMIC CYCLE

The economy continues to change, so specific episodes vary from one to another, but some commonalties of business cycles persist. Profits, for a big example, are far more volatile than overall production. (In this book, I use "volatile" to mean unstable.) A fairly mild recession can send total corporate profits plummeting, while a decent expansion will balloon earnings. Thus, the corporate treasurer or small business owner must not take too much comfort from economists forecasting only a small recession. It's not small if you go out of business. It's wise to think of profits when the news pundits are arguing about slowdowns versus recessions. Economists sometimes foresee a slowing of the economy that may or may not be a recession. Instead of getting caught up in the argument about recession or not, the business manager should understand that even a slower growth rate will typically feed through the economy to weaken corporate profits. This is especially important to the manager who has just borrowed a large sum to build extra capacity to serve what is expected to be rapidly growing demand.

Real GDP and Real Corporate Profits

CHART 2.2

Chart 2.2 shows four-quarter percentage changes in inflation adjusted GDP (the thick line) and corporate profits (the thin line). We will use this format to compare specific sectors with the overall economy. The first thing to examine is the volatility of the lines. Which variable has higher highs and lower lows? Which variable is more stable?

The second thing to look at here is the timing of change. Does one series tend to turn down ahead of the others? Changes in corporate profits are roughly contemporaneous with changes in GDP, but with exceptions in both directions. Other series will have pronounced leads or lags. The third element that we inspect in these charts is the average magnitude of the changes. Is one series, on average, higher than the other? In this example, corporate profits are a little more often above real GDP growth.

Corporate profits are more volatile than the overall economy primarily because costs don't change proportionately with sales. Some costs are fixed, such as depreciation, rent, and administrative staff. Variable costs—those that vary with production levels—are not usually proportional. That is, a 10 percent cut in production cannot always be carried out with a 10 percent cut in staff. There may be some people who have critical skills and must be kept on even though they are not fully utilized. Similarly, a company may keep its more experienced—and higher paid—workers, while letting go the junior employees. That does not bring wage costs down in proportion to the headcount. Also, even in the depths of recession, some businesses are thinking about the future and getting ready to build their markets when the economy recovers. They may accept lower profits in the short term for greater profits in the future. Finally, prices may fall in a recession. If so, a 10 percent cut in unit sales, combined with a 5 percent drop in prices, could mean a 15 percent drop in revenues.

In the following sections, we'll review the major categories of GDP. For each category, we'll assess its stability or volatility, its average growth rate compared to GDP, and the timing of its changes.

KEY POINTS	
Profits fluctuate more than the overall economy, on both the upside and the downside.	In a recession, costs do not fall as much as sales fall, so profits decline.

CONSUMER SPENDING

Consumer spending accounts for about two-thirds of GDP, so it can't rise or fall too much differently than total GDP. However, the record shows that consumer spending does not swing up and down as much as total GDP. Consumers are able to smooth their spending somewhat. For example, in the recession of the early 1980s, consumer spending didn't fall as much as GDP did, and then, in the subsequent recovery, consumer spending didn't rebound as sharply as GDP did. Compare Chart 2.3 below, on consumer spending, with Chart 2.2 on corporate profits. Consumer spending tracks much more closely to GDP than corporate profits do. Note that for the corporate profits chart, we needed a scale running from minus 40 percent to plus 60 percent. For consumer spending, however, our scale need only range from minus 5 percent to plus 15 percent.

In good times, people tend to save a bit more, especially from irregular sources of income, such as bonuses, stock options, and other windfalls. They certainly spend some of the windfall, but it's a smaller percentage than they spend out of their routine monthly income. When incomes fall, consumers don't reduce spending proportionately to their decline in income.

Real GDP and Consumer Spending

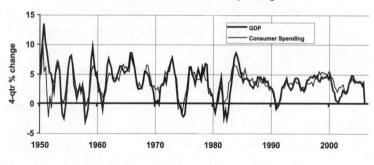

CHART 2.3

Think a little about your own experiences. Have you ever been unemployed? Or, if you're a business owner, have you ever had a really bad year? Did you continue to spend at least a portion of what you usually do? My guess is that you still ate food, still lived in a house or apartment, and still paid the electricity and telephone bills. You may have cut back some, but not proportionately to your decline in income. To do this, you may have used some savings. You may have received unemployment insurance benefits or borrowed money. That's how consumers smooth out spending in the bad times.

If you're a retailer, a manufacturer, or wholesaler of consumer goods, enjoy this good news. You are still subject to recessions, but your experience won't be quite as wild as the overall economy. However, even with consumer spending, the devil is in the details. Your mileage may vary. Nobody really sells all consumer goods and services, so we have to look at specifics. The most stable category of consumer spending is services, which includes items such as utilities, health care, haircuts, and private education.

Health care is the most stable of the services. This may be surprising at first blush, because so many people get their health coverage through their employers. Losing a job may mean losing health insurance. However, there are several stabilizing factors at work. First, a disproportionate amount of health care goes to the elderly, who are not affected by layoffs because they are most likely not employed in the first place. When you hear someone complain about living on a fixed income, you can note that "fixed" also means "not subject to layoff" and "not dependent on the stock market." Second, some people who are laid off in a recession have health insurance through a spouse. Third, many people who are laid off continue their health insurance through COBRA, the law that requires companies to allow former employees to buy health insurance through the company for eighteen months after separation. In addition, Medicaid and other government programs tend to stabilize spending on health care over the business cycle. As a result of these stabilizing factors, health care spending is very stable.

CHART 2.4

Big-ticket discretionary items show the other extreme of consumer spending. The automobile industry is notoriously cyclical. Home electronics, furniture, and, to a lesser extent, clothing, are discretionary purchases that are postponed or downsized in a recession. On the upside, a person with a bonus or unusually large sales commission is more likely to spend the windfall on a car, boat, or vacation than to buy more food and electricity. We call this sector "consumer durables" to reflect that the goods included here last more

BUSINOMICS **THE LUXURY MARKET ISN'T STABLE, EITHER**

▶ Many investors have told me that they have invested in companies that are not vulnerable to recession. Most of these investors have been wrong. One of the more erroneous claims is that "the rich will always have money," so sellers of luxury goods will do just fine. The experience of yacht builders in the early 1990s illustrates the error of this belief. In 1990, the first Bush administration signed into law a tax hike that included a luxury tax on yachts valued over $100,000. The price limit was set to avoid affecting the small fishing boats and runabouts that the middle class likes to own. On the heels of the luxury tax came the 1990–1991 recession.

What happened to the yacht-building industry? It nearly died. Congress had heard testimony that its tax would raise $31 million. It actually only raised $16.6 million, meaning that yacht sales were about half of expectations. The tax caused a loss of 7,600 jobs in the boat-building industry, according to econometric studies of the tax. The total job loss was even greater when the effects of the recession are added in. Maybe the rich will always have money, but they are not always willing to spend it.

The luxury tax was repealed in 1993. The economy recovered, and a yacht-building boom followed. The boat yards that were able to turn out 100-foot yachts were going strong, with order backlogs of several years. The luxury market is vulnerable to the economy and taxes, just like the rest of the economy.

than a year. In contrast, nondurables are used up regularly, including things such as paper towels, gasoline, and food.

Nondurable consumer goods—food, paper products, gasoline, clothing—have intermediate volatility. (Clothing has a spending pattern more like durable goods in terms of sensitivity to recession, though the official government statistics classifies clothing as nondurable goods.)

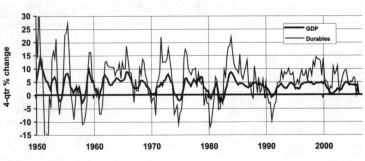

CHART 2.5

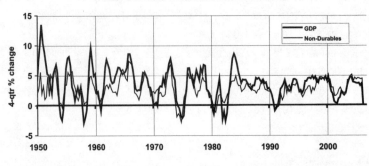

CHART 2.6

KEY POINTS

KEY POINTS		
Consumer services is the most stable part of the economy.	Consumer spending on durable goods, especially big-ticket discretionary purchases, is a highly cyclical sector.	Consumer spending on nondurable goods is more stable than the overall economy, but not enough to be considered recession-proof.

HOUSING

Construction of new housing varies far more widely than does the overall economy, making it one of the most volatile sectors of the economy. Although our need for bedrooms is fairly stable, our need for new bedrooms, and our ability to pay for them, swings around dramatically. Interest rates drive the housing cycle, which in turn drives the overall economic cycle.

One might ask, if housing construction has declined, where do the families live who otherwise would have lived

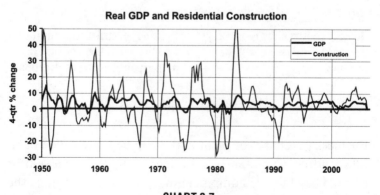

CHART 2.7

in the new housing? It's a good question. The flip side can be asked during a construction boom: Where are the new occupants coming from? The answer to these questions is that some people have a good bit of flexibility in their housing arrangements. Will young adults live with their parents or in their own apartment? If an apartment, will it be occupied by one person or by four roommates? Will the well-to-do family buy a summer home? Will an apartment developer construct a new building in anticipation of future growth? Will there be many vacancies in apartments, or few? The answers to these questions explain how a given housing stock can accommodate more or fewer families.

Housing is a very pronounced leading indicator of the economy. (See the "Jargon Made Clear" box below for more on leading indicators.) When the housing market weakens, it usually does so before the economy as a whole turns down. Similarly, housing is almost always the first sector to recover from recession. In fact, housing sometimes finishes its downturn and starts to improve just as the rest of the economy turns down.

KEY POINTS

Housing construction is one of the most volatile sectors of the economy.	Housing construction tends to lead the rest of the economy, in both expansions and contractions.

CAPITAL SPENDING

Business purchases of plant and equipment are called capital spending. Capital assets, by definition, will last a year or more. They include equipment and software, as well as the buildings in which the equipment are housed.

Capital spending has very wide changes across the business cycle. The peaks run at 20 percent annual growth rates, while the downturns run 10 to 20 percent declines. Individual types of capital spending have far more volatile histories.

BUSINOMICS JARGON MADE CLEAR: *LEADING INDICATORS*

▶ A leading indicator points the way that the rest of the economy will later move in. In contrast, a lagging indicator moves after the economy as a whole has turned.

Economic data that come out over time often fall into one of three categories: leading, coincident, or lagging. Leading indicators tend to move up or down before the overall economy moves up or down. Examples include stock market indexes and housing starts. Coincident indicators tend to move at just the same time as the economy. Examples include employment and industrial production. Finally, lagging indicators, such as commercial and industrial loans, tend to show delayed movement compared to the overall economy.

As an illustration, look at Chart 2.7 on residential construction, which is a leading indicator. Look at the early 1970s. The growth rate of construction began to decline while GDP (the bold line) was still accelerating. When construction growth turned negative, the overall economy was still expanding. That's the concept of a leading indicator.

An index of each type of indicator was developed by the U.S. Department of Commerce, and is now published by a private organization, the Conference Board. When the newspaper headline reads, "Leading Indicators Up for Third Month," the story is reporting that the Conference Board's index of leading indicators has risen. Incidentally, there's enough variation in the data that we economists don't take changes in the leading indicators too seriously until we see three consecutive months of movement in the same direction.

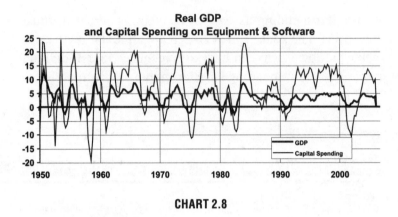

CHART 2.8

Capital spending tends to lag behind the overall business cycle, both on the upside as well as on the downside. This fundamental fact should be understood by anyone selling equipment. Companies purchase equipment to expand capacity or to reduce the cost of producing at the present level of output. Companies buy the most at the peak of the boom, when production is running near full capacity. Purchasing and installing new equipment often entails long lead times, so the spending continues well after the overall business cycle has passed its peak. Similarly, decisions to spend money to reduce production costs are usually made at the peak of the boom when corporate coffers are flush with cash.

On the recovery side of the business cycle, the economy can turn up and actual production will continue to be below installed productive capacity. Think of a company that, at its peak, produced 1,000 pounds of stuff per day, which was their maximum capacity. A recession hits, and demand for stuff falls to 800 pounds per day. Then the recovery begins, and demand rises up to 900 pounds. The economy is in recovery, but this company doesn't need extra capacity. It won't need to expand until demand gets back up to 1,000 pounds. The producers of stuff-making equipment don't get a new order until the recovery has progressed so far that demand approaches its previous peak. In addition, cash positions take a while to rebuild, so corporate treasurers tend to discourage capital spending until a company's balance sheet looks healthy, which will be some time into the recovery.

As a general rule, longer time lags are involved with more expensive and more complex goods. At the extreme end, aircraft production lags well behind the economy, by as much as two years.

I made a very bad economic assessment at the end of 1991. The economy had entered recession in mid-1990, then begun its recovery in the spring of 1991. By December 1991, the economy was growing decently, with more growth likely in 1992. In a speech in Seattle, I said that the Washington economy had dodged a bullet because a recession had come and gone without a drop in Boeing's aircraft employment. The words had hardly left my mouth when the layoffs began. In the next year, the aircraft company's Washington State operations reduced its headcount by 6,000 workers, and they weren't done laying people off until 1995, by which time it had cut 36,000 jobs.

Where did I go wrong? I had underestimated the time lags involved in big-ticket capital goods. I later compared Boeing's history to national economic data and found a time lag that averaged about two years. With such a long time lag, the national recession can be over and done before the aircraft manufacturing industry feels the recession's effects. Commercial airplanes are the most extreme case, but anyone making big, expensive, complicated items should think in terms of long time lags.

The construction side of capital spending—office buildings, stores, and industrial factories—tend to have even greater time lags than equipment because of the longer lead times needed to complete the project. The extreme case is high-rise office buildings, where construction has a very pronounced time lag from the overall business cycle.

GDP and Nonresidential Construction

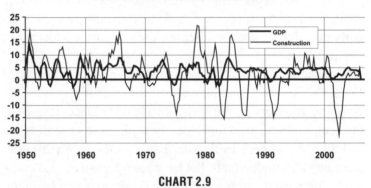

CHART 2.9

KEY POINTS	
Business capital spending is very volatile.	It lags behind the overall economic cycle, with especially long lags for large, big-ticket items with long lead times, such as office buildings and airplanes.

GOVERNMENT SPENDING

Some businesses sell to the government. They will find that federal purchasing varies somewhat more than does the overall economy but that it is not always correlated with the economy. Recessions don't really hurt federal spending because the government can run a deficit. However, weak federal spending can trigger a recession. The reduction in defense spending as the Vietnam War started to taper down was a contributing factor to the 1970 recession. A defense contractor in Southern California would not have expected to be sensitive to recession, but he was certainly sensitive to a decline in military spending. Then, after military spending dropped, the civilian economy was hurting, making it harder to find nonmilitary business. It was not the recession that caused defense contractors to see weak sales, but rather their weak sales that partially caused the recession.

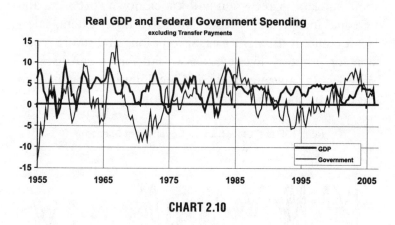

Real GDP and Federal Government Spending
excluding Transfer Payments

CHART 2.10

In Chart 2.10, note that the data begins in 1955. Had we started in 1950, as we did with the other charts, the Korean War would have required the scale go up to 90 percent growth. That would have made it impossible to see any lesser changes, but it's something that should be kept in mind: Wars can make federal spending go bonkers.

Most federal nondefense spending is fairly stable, but program-level spending has substantial ups and downs. For example, it's a good bet that the United States will continue to spend money on environmental cleanup. But that does not mean a specific project will continue. Projects come and go. Sometimes they go because the project has been completed, while at other times projects go because political support has waned.

The use of fiscal policy as a possible means of stabilizing the economy is discussed in Chapter 3.

State and local government spending is more stable than average, but it is still somewhat sensitive to the economy. Most state and local governments are required to balance their budgets. A recession will knock down corporate and personal income-tax revenues and, to a lesser extent, sales-tax revenue. It usually takes a pretty long and severe recession for property tax revenues to fall, but it can happen. With less tax revenue, state and local governments have to cut back on their spending in recessions.

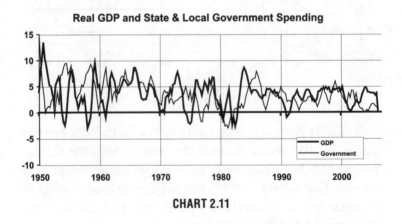

Real GDP and State & Local Government Spending

CHART 2.11

When the first news of a change in revenue hits the state legislature, the elected leaders start wondering what to do.

If the news is good, the politicians begin their public discussions about increasing spending or cutting taxes. If the news is bad, they discuss cutting spending or raising taxes. They will try to reach a political consensus on how to balance the budget. The need for public discussion and perhaps legislative action delays response to revenue changes. As the government nears the end of its budget period, large changes may be implemented. Because of the need for public deliberation, spending changes only take place long after an unanticipated change in revenue.

Local governments vary in their responsiveness to local economic conditions. Property taxes provide most of the fuel for local budgets in most cities, but the responsiveness of tax revenues to the economy varies widely. In some locales, changes in property values translate quickly into changes in revenues. In other places, increases are limited, and tax revenue is much more stable.

Highway funds are usually accounted for separately from the state or local government's general fund. A road-paving contractor, for instance, should understand the appropriations process for the governments he serves. In many states, gasoline tax revenues are placed in a highway trust fund. In this case, revenue available for highways is more stable than revenue for other purposes. First, the gas tax revenue is usually more stable than, say, income tax revenue. Second, highway projects do not have to compete with other government functions because they have that trust fund. For example, legislators in most states cannot cut road work in order to hire more prison guards.

Businesses selling to many different state and local governments can base their decisions on these generalizations. However, those companies selling to just one state (or only a few), as well as the state itself, should understand how that state's revenue structure interacts with the economy to determine revenues.

As a general rule, state sales tax revenue is more stable than state income-tax revenue. The most stable source of revenue is usually property taxes. However, specific rules about exemptions and deductions can add or subtract stability to a state or local tax system, so drilling down to the specific state's tax rules may be necessary.

KEY POINTS

Federal government spending is usually not correlated with economic cycles.	State and local government spending is strongly affected by the economy, with larger effects in states dependent on income taxes. Spending changes are lagged relative to the overall economic cycle.

EXPORTS

Exports are relatively volatile. They are more stable than housing or capital spending but less stable than consumer or government spending. The sharp fluctuations of exports are mitigated, however, by their strong upward trend. Because of the long-term trend toward globalization, U.S. exports and imports have both grown over the last fifty years at a pace far exceeding growth in domestic spending. Exports and imports have also grown faster than any of the major components of domestic spending. In Chart 2.12, note how much of the time the line for exports lies above the line for GDP.

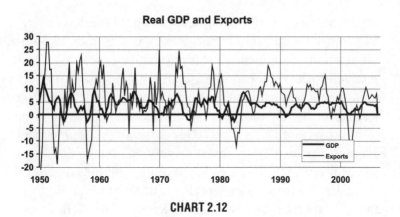

Real GDP and Exports

CHART 2.12

TABLE 2-C

U.S. Merchandise Exports	($ billions)
Capital goods	362
Industrial supplies	232
Consumer goods	116
Automotive vehicles	98
Food, feed, beverages	59
Other goods	39
TOTAL	904

Because of our persistent trade deficit (more imports than exports), many people seem to think that the United States has few exports. That is not at all true. The following table shows nearly $1 trillion worth of exports, even before we count services.

The range of products in exports is staggering. The largest component of capital goods is trucks and car parts. American car companies export parts, such as transmissions, to their overseas operations. Aircraft is another large export category, with Boeing accounting for the lion's share. Electronic equipment, medical equipment, and telecommunications equipment all show up on the export list. Even semiconductors are exported, even though we also import many semiconductors. This is just one category; there is a wide diversity of goods exported.

Who buys all this stuff? Our largest trading partners are—no surprise—our closest neighbors, Canada and Mexico. However, the list spreads out quite a bit outside North America. Our top ten export clients account for about two-thirds of total exports, so there's plenty of room left for the smaller countries. Other than Canada and Mexico, most of our significant trading partners are in Asia and Western Europe.

So what determines the level of our exports? The condition of foreign economies and our exchange rates tend to be the determining factors, so there is not a consistent lead or lag between U.S. exports and U.S. gross domestic product. Exports can drop first, in which case we describe the U.S. downturn as being at least partially caused by foreign weakness. Exports may drop after the U.S. downturn begins, in what we describe as an "echo downturn." Presumably, the U.S. downturn caused our imports to weaken, leading foreign economies to soften, in turn depressing our exports to those economies. Just like the echo in a canyon, an echo downturn is far softer than the initial downturn.

Exports may also be totally impervious to a decline in the U.S. economy if the American decline does not spread to foreign countries. In the 1970 recession, for example, strong exports helped to cushion the drop in domestic spending.

Exports may also decline when the U.S. economy is strong. However, world economies tend to move together. Their patterns do not align perfectly with each other, but there is a loose correlation. As a result, U.S. exports tend to be weak when other parts of the economy are also weak. The correlation, however, is much lower than we would see for consumer spending or capital spending.

Increased economic integration around the world should bring countries into greater synchronization. The data are not yet clearly illustrating the phenomenon, but virtually all business-cycle observers are anticipating closer economic parallels among the nations of the world in the future than we have seen in the past.

KEY POINT

Exports display large swings, but they are not strongly correlated with the American economic cycle.

IMPORTS

Imports in the aggregate fluctuate much more than the overall economy, on a par with exports but with a much stronger correlation to the U.S. economy. It may seem strange that total imports fluctuate more than other types of domestic spending. After all, why should the sale in the United States of imported cars be more variable than the sale of domestic cars? The answer is that we tend to import goods for which we have volatile spending patterns. We tend not to import the things on which our spending is very stable.

Real GDP and Exports

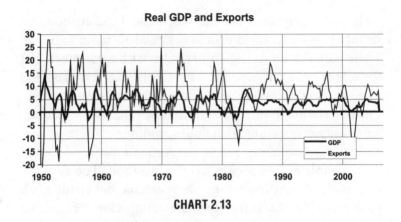

CHART 2.13

My haircut is not a cheap imported haircut (even if my friends tell me that it looks like one). My electricity and water are not imported. My health care is not imported. These are all relatively stable parts of my spending.

On the other hand, we import plenty of the goods in our most volatile sector of consumer spending: durable goods, such as cars and electronic equipment. The United States also imports a good deal of apparel, the most volatile part of consumer nondurable goods spending. American businesses import much equipment, as most any factory tour will show. Thus, the kind of goods that we import tend to be unstable over time, so our imports tend to be volatile.

For a business importing goods into the United States, it's more important to look at the type of spending that the goods represent, rather than the fact that they are imported. The same holds true for transportation companies and related service businesses, such as freight forwarders, which depend on import volumes for profitability.

Demand for imports varies with the underlying
domestic demand for that type of good or service.

SUMMING UP

The business implication of this discussion of timing and
magnitude of spending changes is that you have to know
who your customers are, and perhaps who their customers are, in order to assess your own sensitivity to recession.
When managing a business, you have to look at *your* sales
and determine whether they are relatively volatile or relatively stable. You should also determine whether there are
leads or lags between your sales and the overall economy.

BUSINOMICS

How to Anticipate Recessions and Downturns

WILLIAM B. CONERLY, PH.D.—In the early summer of 1990, the economy was slowing down as the Federal Reserve raised interest rates. I had forecast a further slowing of economic growth rates but no recession. Then I took off on a raft trip down the Grand Canyon, where I was totally out of touch with the news.

After two weeks of a great vacation, we left the canyon and flew into Las Vegas, dirty and relaxed. On the newsstands, I saw curious headlines. Iraqi troops were in Kuwait. The United States was mobilizing forces to be sent to Saudi Arabia. It was time to hurry back to the office and reevaluate the forecast.

Columnists who are generally ignorant of economics will write that war is good for the economy. The first Gulf War triggered a recession, which isn't good for most businesses. Consumer confidence fell, as did business confidence. In the autumn of 1990, I met with many business managers and probed for their responses to the war. Most of the executives were running their businesses pretty much as they had previously planned, but they were nervous. Perhaps one in five or one in ten was delaying spending plans. They didn't overreact (they thought) and cancel projects. They just decided to "wait and see" how the war affected the economy. Business orders for capital goods dropped 16 percent from July through November of 1990. The businesses that were delaying their spending felt that they were only making a small adjustment. The businesses that were selling equipment, however, felt a whopping slap across their faces.

Consumers had been slowing their discretionary spending before the invasion of Kuwait, as a result of the Fed's past tightening. (There's a long time lag between cause and effect in monetary policy.) Consumers really pulled in their horns late in 1990, as the impending battle brought consumer confidence down sharply, cutting retail spending by about 3 percent. This is a lot less than the percentage drop in business spending, but remember that consumer spending far exceeds the dollars spent by businesses on capital equipment.

While all of this was going on, the thrift industry (savings-and-loan associations and mutual savings banks) was collapsing from previous problems, compounded by the Fed's increase in interest rates. Furthermore, a commercial real estate bubble was bursting. The invasion of Kuwait happened about the same time that nonresidential construction peaked. In twelve months' time, commercial and industrial construction dropped by 25 percent. Part of this was due to past overbuilding and part due to a credit crunch. Banks were severely criticized by regulators over their real estate lending and were forced to write down or write off many loans. In this environment, lending on new projects came to a screeching halt.

So what caused this recession? Monetary policy is always my favorite culprit, and in this case, the Fed had in fact raised interest rates prior to the recession. But the collapse of business and consumer confidence caused by the Gulf War buildup probably pushed us over the brink. The real estate problems and the thrift industry crisis also contributed to the downturn.

One problem may remove the economy's "cushion" or margin for error, allowing a second or third problem to be the straw that breaks the economy's back. Here, in this chapter, I'll present the leading straws, in their order of importance.

WHAT REALLY CAUSES RECESSIONS?

To anticipate a recession or downturn, a business leader must understand the causes of recessions and downturns. However, the knowledge about causes that you need as a business manager is somewhat different from the knowledge needed by an economic theorist or a policymaker. A business leader needs to know the signals of impending recessions and downturns. Academic theorists can look for elegant theories, and policymakers can study how to prevent or mitigate recessions. For a business, though, the crucial knowledge is what signals are given off by an economy nearing recession.

This chapter might be titled "Causes of Recession," were it not for two elements. First, we will relentlessly focus on observable signs of future changes. Second, when discussing various causes, we will also discuss which causes come up most often and which are rare. This means that you can make sure to put on your radar screen the signals that most commonly predict future recessions and downturns.

Simple theories of recession don't work very well because multiple strains on an economy often trigger the actual recession. One strain may not be enough to push the economy into a downturn, but the addition of other strains pushes the economy over the brink. The 1990–1991 recession was a good case in point.

Monetary policy is the most common cause of recession, with supply shocks (sudden increases in the price of oil or other key goods) a distant second. In addition to these two, there are numerous other problems that can add strain to a weakening economy and help trigger an actual recession.

"Simple theories of recession don't work very well because multiple strains on an economy often trigger the actual recession."

In the 1960s, controversy raged within the economics profession between the Keynesians and the monetarists. I take a generally monetarist point of view, but with a strong appreciation for many of Keynes's insights. The following section takes up the nuts and bolts of the causes of recession, but first we need a short explanation of how we got to this viewpoint.

Classical economists—those before Keynes—generally thought that the economy would be self-regulating. But the Great Depression sure didn't look like an economy doing a good job of regulating itself, and that lead John Maynard Keynes to develop his theory of business cycles. He said that some business decisions, such as capital spending, don't have a very firm foundation because so little is known about future economic conditions. Business leaders tend to move together in waves of optimism or pessimism, causing boom-bust cycles. This view held sway from its publication in 1936 until the 1960s.

Milton Friedman led a monetarist attack on the Keynesian view, arguing instead that monetary policy—changes in the money supply—was the primary cause of business cycles. At the same time, other theorists were noting that some very restrictive assumptions were needed to make a theoretical model of the economy behave in a Keynesian way.

Many politicians embraced the Keynesian view because it justified a larger government budget. They seldom recalled that Keynes had recommended running budget surpluses during good times. In practice, fine-tuning the economy with fiscal policy proved impractical.

At this stage, most (though not all) economists acknowledge the significance of monetary policy. Many also acknowledge that the economy will be impacted by fiscal policy and various other shocks. The explanation that follows is near the mainstream, but with a larger role for monetary policy and a smaller role for fiscal policy than the average economist might give.

Before discussing these potential causes of recession, a reality check is in order. More often than not, the economy is expanding. Growth is the norm, and recession is the exception. The discussion of recessions is important because of the danger they pose to business survival, but leaders should not become preoccupied with downside risk. That's like spending a vacation drive worrying about having an accident. Consider the possibility, buckle your seat belts, then have a great time.

MONETARY POLICY

The Federal Reserve influences both the money supply (the number of dollars circulating in the form of currency or bank account balances) and short-term interest rates. Sometimes the Fed focuses on money supply, and sometimes on interest rates, but the result is that when the Fed tightens (slows growth of the money supply and raises interest rates), the economy slows down.

Milton Friedman and Anna Schwartz's classic work, *A Monetary History of the United States: 1867 to 1960*, laid out the case for monetary policy as the major force in the business cycle. Their thesis was not well received at first, coming in the heyday of Keynesian policy. But over time, economists have come to regard Friedman and Schwartz's approach as basic to an understanding of business cycles. Friedman won a Nobel Prize partly for this work.

Business leaders need to understand the direction and magnitude of Fed policy. They can, however, skip over many of the theoretical issues considered by professional economists. The press pretty well covers the obvious parts of Fed policy: whether short-term interest rates are up or down. The first step, then, is to watch the Fed Funds rate, which is the interest rate on overnight loans among banks. Data are available on a daily basis from the Federal Reserve, but it's enough to keep an eye on the newspaper for announcements of Fed policy changes.

In the past, watching changes in the money supply was the best way to track monetary policy. In the 1980s, for example,

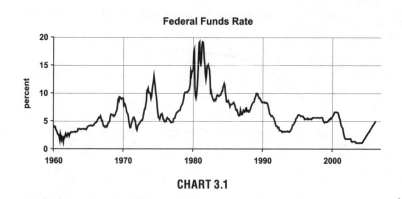

Federal Funds Rate

CHART 3.1

the Fed's weekly report on the money supply moved markets. Today, however, few economists monitor money supply. First, we no longer need indirect measures of the Fed's intentions. The Federal Reserve Board has decided to announce its policies in clear terms. Second, money supply has become a very difficult tool for gauging Fed policy. Sweep accounts (in which a company's bank deposits are swept into an investment account every night) have distorted the money supply statistics so that they are not as reliable as they used to be. And plenty of economists had, in the past, observed that money supply was not perfectly reliable. So at this time, it's best to watch short-term interest rates to gauge monetary policy and thus the potential for an economic slowdown.

The yield curve is also a good indicator of the direction of monetary policy. A yield curve shows interest rates by maturity. Most of the time, long-term interest rates are higher than short-term interest rates. That is, a government bond that matures in ten years will pay a higher annual interest rate than a treasury bill that matures in a year or less. Chart 3.2 shows a typical yield curve. This is from the first month of expansion after the 2001 recession was over.

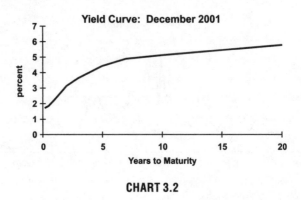

CHART 3.2

When the short-term interest rate is higher than the long-term interest rate, the yield curve is said to be inverted, or downward sloping. This is a sign that the Fed is tightening, or has tightened. It's also a good sign that the economy will slow down. Chart 3.3 shows the yield curve three months prior to the beginning of the 1980 recession. A full-blown recession does not necessarily follow an inversion of the yield curve, but at least a slowing of the economy's growth rate is certain.

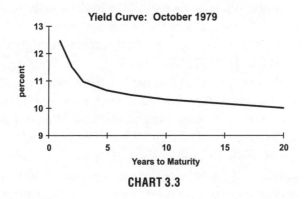

CHART 3.3

At times of extreme conditions, interest rates don't tell an accurate story. That was true in the Great Depression and in Japan in the 1990s. When inflation is declining to near zero, or actually turning to deflation (prices going down), then falling interest rates may not indicate that the central bank is easing. ("Central bank" is the generic term for national monetary institutions such as the Federal Reserve.) The crucial issue is not interest rates per se, but "real" interest rates.

A real interest rate is the "nominal" or ordinary interest rate minus the inflation rate. In 1977, for example, the interest rate on treasury bills ("T-bills") was just over 6 percent, which seemed high at the time. But inflation was also about

6 percent. Thus, the purchasing power of dollars lent out matched the purchasing power of the dollars that were to be repaid. In effect, loans were free.

The opposite occurred in Japan's recession. In 2000 and 2001, Japanese interest rates were just above zero, so it appeared that loans were nearly free. However, prices were falling, at times by more than 1 percent per year. Real interest rates were thus about 1 percent. That's not nearly as cheap as real interest rates had been in Japan in 1997. So instead of providing further stimulus to the economy, Japanese monetary policy had tightened up. Similarly, during our Great Depression, real interest rates were higher than nominal rates. In 1932, the interest rate on Treasury Bills was just 0.9 percent. That sounds low. However, prices were declining by about 10 percent. The lender was repaid in dollars of much higher purchasing power and came out ahead by about 11 percent. Now that's a high interest rate!

At times of low inflation, you need to look at money supply. Even though it's not a perfect gauge of monetary policy, it is the only way to see what is happening during times of deflation. For instance, in the aftermath of the 1929 stock market crash, interest rates fell—but the money supply dropped by one-third. Usually, interest rates move in the

BUSINOMICS JARGON MADE CLEAR: *REAL INTEREST RATES*

▶ The "real" in this term means "inflation adjusted." A real interest rate is the interest rate minus the rate of inflation. This gives us the genuine cost of borrowing, taking into account that the dollars paid back will have a different purchasing power than the dollars originally borrowed.

opposite direction from changes in the money supply. But with falling prices and falling demand for credit, nominal interest rates fell and real interest rates rose, even though the money supply was contracting. The Fed did not understand that it was tightening monetary policy—as shown by the falling money supply—and thereby causing the recession to become a depression.

Japan, similarly, viewed its monetary policy in the 1990s as loose because interest rates were so low, but without realizing that their money supply growth had really been weak. Flood the economy with money, Friedman observed, and the economy will get going. Japan eventually proved this point, implementing a policy they called "quantitative easing," meaning that they continued to increase their money supply even after interest rates were nearly zero.

The savvy business manager should watch monetary policy by noticing Fed policy announcements in the news, keeping an eye on the Fed Funds rate, and monitoring the yield curve. In severe recessions, the manager must watch the money supply more than interest rates.

Time Lags

Now for the hard part: time lags. Friedman concluded that the time lags in monetary policy are "long and variable." Here's a general rule of thumb that I use: The effects of monetary policy on spending, employment, and production take six to twelve months to be felt, with another twelve months before inflation reacts. Other economists, however, have come up with estimates shorter or longer than my range, so some skepticism is justified. The important point is not to expect immediate results from the Fed's action.

Reading the daily newspapers or watching the nightly news will not help one understand time lags. I've had a reporter call me the day after the Fed changed interest rates, asking, "Have you seen any effect of the Federal Reserve's rate cut yet?" My usual response is "Huh?" It takes six to twelve months to see an effect, so I can go on vacation for a good long time before I need to start looking for signs that the Fed has affected the economy.

This desire for instant gratification causes a misplaced sense that monetary policy is not effective. After all, the thinking goes, if we haven't seen an effect in a few weeks or a few months, then why should we think that we'll ever see an effect? The answer is that a bit of study shows that monetary policy works, but with long time lags. Chart 3.4 illustrates the long time lags involved. After policy is changed, quite a bit of time goes by before the effects are seen.

Monetary Policy

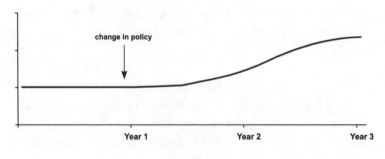

CHART 3.4

Fed policy changes tend to be incremental, further lengthening the time lags. When the Fed raises the Fed Funds rate by 25 basis points (100 basis points equals 1 percentage point), not much happens. When the Fed raises (or lowers) rates by 2 or 3 full percentage points, things certainly happen. But the Fed usually spreads such moves over many months. The Fed's action in 2001 is typical. Policy had been stable in the second half of 2000. Then the Fed saw signs of economic weakness (well before September 11) and eased. The Fed moved interest rates down incrementally over the course of the year, then stabilized the Fed Funds rate and waited for the policy to take effect.

Federal Funds Rate: 2000–2002

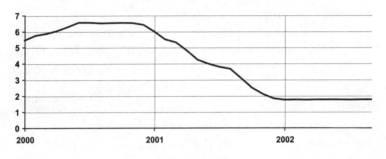

CHART 3.5

BUSINOMICS HOW THE FED CONDUCTS MONETARY POLICY

▶ The Federal Reserve makes monetary policy decisions primarily through its Federal Open Market Committee (FOMC). The group consists of the seven governors of the Fed, plus four of the twelve presidents of the regional Federal Reserve banks. The chairman of the Fed is often thought to make the decisions, but in reality he or she has to gain the support of the committee. Sometimes that support is granted out of respect for the chairman, but generally the chairman has to persuade the committee. The actual conduct of monetary policy involves the Federal Reserves security trading-desk buying or selling treasury bills to peg the short-term interest rate at the committee's targeted level.

THE PROCESS OF MONETARY RECESSIONS

The process whereby Fed policy is translated into a business slowdown or recession is important to managers—because it's being translated through you! Lightning is simply a movement of electrical charges from the sky to the ground. But if it's going through your body, you have more than an academic interest in the phenomenon. Similarly, if lower sales at your company constitute the Fed's "monetary policy transmission mechanism," then you had better understand what is happening.

The seeds of a recession or slowdown induced by monetary policy usually sprout in the fertile soil of a boom. Business is strong, and the Fed initially is hesitant to quiet the party. Everyone's having so much fun! Why spoil it? But eventually the Fed worries about inflation. The Fed may be seeing actual signs of inflation, or the Fed may be anticipating inflation. Remember, the time lag between Fed policy and inflation is twelve to twenty-four months, so the Fed looks ahead. You may not be seeing inflation in the prices you can charge your customers or in the prices you pay to your vendors, but that doesn't mean the Fed isn't worrying about inflation in the future. If they believe that their current policy would lead to higher inflation in the coming year, they'll usually begin tightening now.

The Basic Recession Time Line

Rising interest rates → Home sales decline → Housing starts decline → Construction employment declines → Other interest-sensitive spending declines → Cars sales decline → Some capital spending declines → Employment in construction and manufacturing declines → Consumer spending declines → Inventories decline → Production declines again

➔ Manufacturing decline spreads through economy ➔ Capital spending falls ➔ Interest rates fall due to weak demand for credit and Fed easing ➔ Prices of some interest-sensitive products (houses, cars) fall ➔ Consumers who have reliable incomes increase spending ➔ Production of interest-sensitive products increases ➔ Housing sales and starts increase ➔ Employment in construction and manufacturing increases ➔ Inventories are increased ➔ Capital spending increases

As interest rates rise, homebuilding starts to slow down, as do other interest-sensitive sectors of the economy, such as automobile sales. Homebuilding is usually the first sector to slow down in a recession. It is the ultimate interest-sensitive item. Cars and light trucks are almost as interest-sensitive, so auto sales tend to decline before the rest of the economy enters the downturn. Some business capital spending is also interest sensitive and will slow down. The rise in interest rates in the United States may push the dollar exchange rate up against foreign currencies. When the dollar rises, U.S.-made goods are more expensive to foreigners: They buy less from us, and our exports decline. The strength of the dollar also makes imports look cheaper to us. We buy more foreign goods in place of merchandise made in America. For all of these reasons, Americans spend less on goods and services made here.

As sales slow down in several sectors, inventories start to build up. Inventory changes are very destabilizing to the economy. This is especially important to keep in mind if your business is some ways distant from the final consumer. The role of inventories in destabilizing the economy can be readily seen in the 2001 recession. Remember that GDP consists of actual spending, plus the change in inventories. The logic is that all goods produced are either bought or added to inventories. The following chart shows real final sales and inventory change. (*Final sales* consists of consumer spending, investment, government spending, and net exports.) Looking only at real final sales, it's not worth calling this episode a recession. But the inventory drawdown had a very pronounced, negative effect, pulling the entire economy into recession.

Real Final Sales and Inventory Change

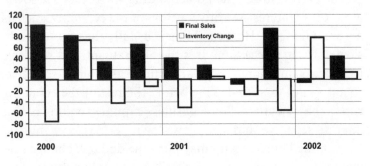

CHART 3.6

Magnified Effects on the Supply Chain

Consider an example with a product close to my heart: beer. Construction workers aren't quite as busy because of the higher interest rates, so they cut back on their beer consumption. (You may actually assume the opposite is true, but according to the data, alcohol consumption goes *down* when unemployment rises.) Let's say that beer consumption falls by 2 percent.

Back up a moment and look at the retailer before the slowdown, as shown in the table below. The beer retailer has been buying as much beer as he sells, keeping his inventory at, let's say, four times weekly sales. He cruises along in a fixed pattern for the first four weeks we look at. His sales are steady at 100 cases a week. At the end of each week, his inventory is down to 300 cases. Given his target inventory-to-sales ratio of four, and his sales of 100, he wants to have 400 cases in inventory. He needs to purchase 100 cases to have an inventory-after-purchase of 400 cases.

In week five, though, those construction workers cut back on their drinking. Sales at the local convenience store fall 2 percent, which doesn't sound like much, but there's a

TABLE 3-A. Beer Sales and Inventory

	Sales	% Change	Inventory after Sales	Target Inventory Ratio	Target Inventory	Purchase	Inventory after Purchases
RETAILER							
Week 1	100		300	4	400	100	400
Week 2	100	0%	300	4	400	100	400
Week 3	100	0%	300	4	400	100	400
Week 4	100	0%	300	4	400	100	400
Week 5	98	-2%	302	4	392	90	392
WHOLESALER (SERVES 100 RETAILERS)							
Week 1	10,000		20,000	3	30,000	10,000	30,000
Week 2	10,000	0%	20,000	3	30,000	10,000	30,000
Week 3	10,000	0%	20,000	3	30,000	10,000	30,000
Week 4	10,000	0%	20,000	3	30,000	10,000	30,000
Week 5	9,000	-10%	21,000	3	27,000	6,000	27,000
BREWER (SERVES 50 RETAILERS)							
Week 1	500,000		500,000	2	1,000,000	500,000	1,000,000
Week 2	500,000	0%	500,000	2	1,000,000	500,000	1,000,000
Week 3	500,000	0%	500,000	2	1,000,000	500,000	1,000,000
Week 4	500,000	0%	500,000	2	1,000,000	500,000	1,000,000
Week 5	300,000	-40%	700,000	2	600,000	-100,000	600,000

real problem brewing. Look first at the retailer's inventory after sales; it's 302 cases, two more than usual. But that's not all. At the lower level of sales, his target inventory has dropped to 392 cases (sales of 98 times the target inventory ratio of 4). So the retailer only purchases ninety cases from his wholesaler.

Look at what happened. A *2 percent* decline in retail sales triggered a *10 percent* decline in wholesale purchases. Yowzah!

We're even being conservative in assuming that the retailer keeps his same old target inventory ratio. The retailer determines this ratio based on the variability of his sales, and the variety of beer brands and sizes that he has to stock to meet customer demand. The inventory target, however, is also influenced by the retailer's financial condition. With sales off, the business may be short of working capital. At a higher interest rate, the decision about how much working capital to tie up in inventories may swing toward leaner stocking of the shelves. So the retailer might have to trim the target inventory ratio, which would cause an even greater decline in purchases from the wholesaler.

In the next section of the table, we show a similar chart for the wholesaler. We assume that the wholesaler serves 100 retailers and has a target inventory ratio of 3. (Some of the ups and downs from individual retailers offset each other, so the wholesaler can get by with a lower inventory-to-sales ratio than the retailers.)

The beer wholesaler sees the 10 percent drop in sales—which was not expected—and cuts back on its purchases from the brewery. The wholesaler has in stock an extra 1,000 cases that normally would have been sold already. Furthermore, the target inventory at the new sales rate is only 27,000 cases. The result? The wholesaler's order to the brewery is for only 6,000 cases, a 40 percent reduction from normal.

The brewer sees the 40 percent decline in sales, and not only cuts back on production, but lowers the inventory of unfinished goods: yeast, hops, and whatever else is in the beer. The brewery also cuts back on purchases of bottles and labels.

So far, the 2 percent decline in final sales has triggered a 40 percent decline in brewery sales, plus an even greater decline in purchases by the brewery. As we continue to go up the supply chain, the effect continues to be magnified. The result of this process is that inventory swings are very destabilizing to the overall economy.

In this simplified example, the entire downward adjustment takes place in one week. Actually, it will be months before all businesses involved realize that their sales are down and that their target inventory levels need to be adjusted.

"The executive needs to understand where the business lies on the supply chain."

The executive needs to understand where the business lies on the supply chain. If the business is close to the final customer, such as the retailer in our beer example, it may not feel as much pain. However, the retailer also gets very little warning about a downturn. Wholesalers who are in close contact with their retailers may see the sales decline unfold with enough warning that they can adjust more gradually. Even before the retailer places his end-of-the-week order, the wholesaler knows what is coming. Manufacturers often have even more lead time, though they are at much greater risk because the reduction in their orders is so much greater, on a percentage basis, than for retailers and wholesalers.

The inventory problem has been reduced by innovations in sales technology. Barcode scanning enables retailers to transmit sales data to wholesalers and manufacturers, daily or even in real time. After collecting some history, wholesalers and manufacturers can identify changing trends on a timely basis. This is one factor likely to reduce the magnitude of recessions—but don't expect recessions to be totally eliminated.

A Widening Slowdown

At this point, the slowdown in construction has spread to consumer goods and to upstream producers of basic commodities (glass and hops). Layoffs in these industries have led consumers to tighten their belts. Some workers are laid off, while others are getting nervous. Now it's not just the construction workers who cut back on their spending, but a much broader cross-section of the population. Spending cuts lead to further layoffs.

Business is slow, and companies start to postpone planned capital expenditures. It may take years to plan a major expansion at a manufacturing plant, but it doesn't take too long to scrub the project when the economy softens. Our moderate decline in production of beer may mean a virtual standstill in the installation of new brewing equipment. Certainly the brewery will rethink its need for additional capacity.

In some industries, optimistic expectations of future growth may drive the capital spending plans even in the face of a downturn. That only occurs when the company has the financial resources to spend on new equipment even as sales are falling. Another requirement is that the capital spending project has a long lead time to completion. If the brewery, for example, is considering a project that can be completed in three months from commitment, then it will most likely wait until it sees demand heading up. If the project, on the other hand, will take three years, then the company has to anticipate sales long into the future. Few companies have both the strong financial resources and the very long lead times necessary for capital expenditures to be impervious to the business cycle. Even if the company is optimistic about the long run and has substantial financial resources, it may think that a little delay, rather than an outright cancellation, is appropriate. The result? Business spending on new buildings, equipment, and software declines markedly in recession.

Some of the planned capital spending may not have been for the purpose of adding new capacity but rather to lower production costs through more efficient equipment. However, it's time for the chief financial officer to speak up. The CFO worries about cash flow. Even if a planned expenditure will pay for itself over time, the CFO must be concerned about the upfront expense. The finance staff will sketch out cash receipts and cash expenditures and run a pessimistic scenario. They will then double-check the company's credit facilities to ensure that the firm will be able to meet payroll and other bills every month. The CFO may decide that the proposed expenditure would take away too much liquidity. A postponement, but not a downright elimination, may be the CFO's suggestion to the chief executive officer.

Pity now the poor manufacturer of the brewing equipment. Equipment sales may be down by 50 percent or more, just because of a silly little 2 percent drop in beer sales. It's temporary, of course, but that's not much comfort to the boss who has to lay off workers because there are not enough orders to keep all of them busy or enough revenue to cover their paychecks.

Effects Throughout the Economy

The general weakening of the economy has now spread from housing construction to consumer goods to capital goods. Cutbacks occur at business services firms, including staffing companies, advertising agencies, law firms, and accountants.

Demand for office space stops rising and begins to decline. The problem with office space, however, it that it takes several years for a high rise to be completed. As the downturn starts, different projects are in a variety of stages, ranging from groundbreaking to completion of interior improvements. In most cases, it makes sense to go ahead and finish the building, adding more space to an already glutted market.

Let's look at what happens to excess inventory. If the inventory consists of bananas, the retailer just waits five days and the problem goes away on its own. The retailer has lost money on his rotten inventory, but now the market is cleared of excess inventory and can move forward. If the inventory is hardware, production is cut back to a level a little less than current consumption, and the excess is soon worked off. It isn't too long before the market is back to normal. But if the inventory is office space, more office space continues to come on the market for two years because of the buildings that had just been started when the recession began. The continued addition of new office space during the recession further accentuates the glut on the commercial real estate market.

This recession has now spread through most of the economy. Everyone knows that the recession is here, and the Fed has begun cutting interest rates. On the government side, Congress and the president start talking about a stimulus package, such as tax cuts and increased spending.

For state and local governments, though, just the opposite is happening. Remember that state and local governments have long time lags before they react to unexpected changes in revenue, due to the need for deliberation and compromise in public policy. Thus, spending continues to grow even as revenues start to decline. As governments near the end of their budget periods, though, draconian measures may be needed to stem the tide of red ink. Remember that most state and local governments must run balanced budgets every year. Eventually, then, state and local governments may enact hiring freezes or even layoffs, and they will delay discretionary expenditures. Taxes may also be increased through temporary surtaxes or even permanent tax hikes.

The Process of Recovery

Consumers have, in general, cut back their spending, but some anomalies can be seen. We tend to think of typical consumers and ask how anyone could make a major purchase, such as a car, when layoffs are increasing. The answer is that we have a great variety of experience among consumers. Some are retired, living on fixed incomes. That's great when the economy is in recession. The car dealers start offering better deals, so some retired person accelerates a planned car purchase to take advantage of the sale. My mail carrier's job isn't subject to the ebbs and tides of layoff, so he too may do more shopping when there are more sales. My dentist need not worry about losing her job, and her view is substantiated by the comments in the previous chapter about the stability of health-care spending. Thus, the economy won't come to an absolute screeching halt, even if it does slow down.

Even before the Fed starts to ease, credit markets are feeling the marked lack of demand for loans. Business borrowing is driven by three key elements: financing inventories, accounts receivables, and capital spending. Remember that businesses are cutting back on inventory and delaying capital spending plans. With lower sales, they have lower accounts receivable. All told, businesses don't need as much credit as they did during the boom. Finally, the decline in construction activity reduces the demand for real estate loans. All combined, the falling demand for credit tends to reduce interest rates.

And then the Fed steps in. They realize that they overdid the tightening and that it is time for easy money. Money-supply growth accelerates, interest rates fall—and not much happens. At least, not at first. The most reliable economic phenomenon after the Fed's first round of interest cuts is an article in the *Wall Street Journal* or the *New York Times* alleging that monetary policy no longer works. The article will cite various structural changes to the economy but totally ignore the long time lags between cause and effect.

Housing will start to rebound as low interest rates spur some folks to buy new houses. Remember the people with secure incomes, such as government and health-care workers? Some of them will take advantage of low interest rate loans and buy new houses. The construction workers go back to work and start buying more beer.

Lower mortgage interest rates are not only stimulating new home sales, they are also leading homeowners to refinance their mortgages at lower interest rates. For some, their monthly payment is reduced, giving them more discretionary income to spend. This income will gradually fuel spending growth. Others see that they can take out a larger mortgage with the same monthly payments, thanks to the lower interest rate. The larger mortgage allows them to put some cash in their pocket, in what's called a cash-out refinancing. These are easier after a period of strong price appreciation, but some cycles and some markets enjoy appreciation even in the depths of the recession. The money gained in the cash-out refinancing is often plowed back into the home in the form of home remodeling. Finally, some homeowners refinance with the same monthly payment to shorten their loan's maturity. In all three cases, the homeowners feel better about their current situation and should be more inclined to spend. This is especially true of the cash-out refinancers, but is also true, to a lesser extent, for the others.

The bars and retailers are running short of beer now. Sales are higher than expected, so inventories are lower than desired. The retailers order not only as much as they sold, they order a little extra to bring their inventories up to the new target inventory level. Just as the retailer's order to the wholesaler was magnified in the down stage of the cycle, the order swing will be magnified on the up stage. The retailer may see only a 2 percent sales gain, but he will boost his order by 10 percent so that inventory gets up to the new target inventory-to-sales ratio. The wholesaler bumps up his order to the brewer, who increases his order with the glass company, and most of the economy gets back to work.

By extending our earlier inventory table, we can graph the variations in sales at retail, wholesale, and manufacturer levels.

After housing, discretionary consumer spending tends to be the next sector to recover. Automobile sales also benefit

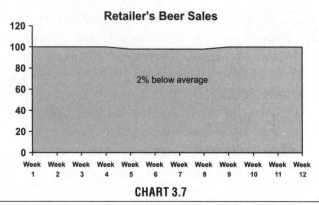

CHART 3.7

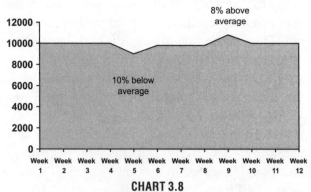

CHART 3.8

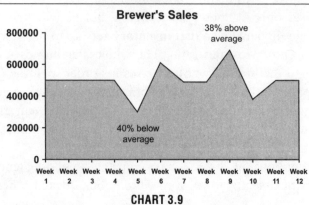

CHART 3.9

from lower interest rates, though not as much as home sales do. Other big-ticket items, such as home electronics, regain ground as employment and incomes recover. Furniture sees a boost, partly from the normal recovery process but also because of the new homebuilding. There's nothing like a new house to trigger a need for new furniture. Garden centers also benefit from new homeowners putting in new lawns, trees, and shrubbery.

Sales of other consumer goods will improve, but not as dramatically. Nondurable goods and services tend to be more stable, and that applies to the recovery as well as to the recession. Look for some improvement, but not a huge increase.

Where's the federal government in all of this? When the recession looks like it is about to end, Congress panics. The end to a recession must be accompanied by an economic stimulus package enacted by Congress and signed by the president. If the stimulus package isn't passed, how can Congress and the president take credit for ending the recession? Sometimes the recession's end creeps up on Congress and nearly catches members unaware. Debate is closed, Democrats come together with Republicans, and a law is passed. The substance of the law is irrelevant to the economy, but it's very important to the reelection bids of everyone involved.

Sometimes the politicians are really slow. John F. Kennedy ran for office during the 1960 recession. He proposed a tax cut after the recession was well over. Congress dithered but finally passed the bill after Kennedy's assassination. The lower tax rates went into effect just as the economy was starting to overheat from easy Fed policy and the Vietnam War. It's hard to be too skeptical about the government's fiscal policy.

More recently, Congress passed tax cuts in 2003 to help stimulate the economy. One feature was a mailing out of anticipated refunds in the third quarter, even before people had filed tax returns for the year. At the same time, withholding schedules were changed to put more money into worker's take-home paychecks. However, this stimulus hit consumers just as everything else was rebounding. Business spending on equipment and software grew by 15 percent that quarter, the best growth rate in over three years. Exports, which had declined for most of the past three years, came roaring back with a double-digit growth rate, thanks to strong growth overseas. In short, the federal government added fiscal stimulus when we finally didn't need it. The result was an unsustainable spike in GDP growth.

Real GDP Growth: 2002–2004

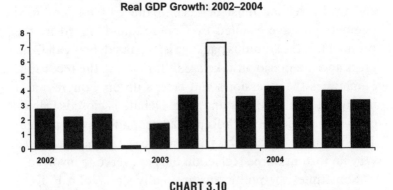

CHART 3.10

Fiscal policy (changes in government spending and taxes) gets a great deal of attention, despite the problems with its timing. The economic profession is still divided between monetarists, who think that monetary policy is the main driver, and the more Keynesian economists, who ascribe a significant role to fiscal policy. I began my forecasting career as a hard-core monetarist but gradually changed my position as a result of watching the quarter-by-quarter movements in the economy.

My conclusion is that over a quarter or two, fiscal policy has a significant effect on the economy, but that effect is offset within a year. For time horizons over one year, I'm still a monetarist, but my very short-term forecast tends to be somewhat Keynesian.

One traditional bit of fiscal policy to be aware of is automatic stabilizers. Even if Congress is dithering about a tax cut or spending increase, stimulus is in the works. Government transfer payments increase during a recession. Unemployment insurance goes up, of course, and more people take early retirement, triggering Social Security payments. On the tax side, people fall into lower tax brackets during the recession, lowering taxes in total and also lowering taxes as a percentage of income. These automatic stabilizers also work in a boom to limit the growth of the economy.

Back to our story: The economy is improving, and maybe the federal government has helped it along with fiscal policy. An upward inventory swing helps the companies producing basic and intermediate goods. Remember the bottle supplier to the brewery, and the label printer? They are seeing better sales now.

Capital goods are slower to recover, waiting until months after the recession is over. Even after overall sales in the economy turn up, total production is likely to still be below the level that triggers a need for additional capacity. Also, CFOs really want to see cash flow improving before they give the green light to the long-delayed spending plans.

Nonresidential construction will be the last of the private sectors to turn around. The office-building market has such long lead times that it takes years to work off the excess supply of space that typically develops in the recession.

The basic business cycle, triggered by monetary policy that is too tight, begins with a mild downturn in housing construction, leading to a mild contraction in consumer spending, which in turn leads to an inventory correction and a severe reduction in capital expenditures. Eventually, low interest rates and prices stimulate spending from income-secure consumers, prompting an inventory rebound, a more general business expansion, and finally the recovery of capital spending.

The recovery comes from a mixture of natural resiliency and policy management. The resiliency is manifested in lower interest rates and lower prices stimulating spending. Policy help comes primarily from monetary policy, if the Fed is doing its job, and possibly from fiscal policy.

KEY POINTS		
Error in monetary policy is the most common cause of recession.	Monetary policy works with long time lags.	A monetary policy–induced recession moves through interest-sensitive sectors of the economy and then spreads throughout the entire economy, but interest rates eventually drop, leading to recovery.

SUPPLY SHOCKS

In October 1973, Egyptian forces attacked the Israeli army in the Sinai Peninsula. Simultaneously, Syria attacked Israeli army units in the Golan Heights. The Soviet Union provided support to the Arabs, while the United States supported Israel. The members of the Organization of Petroleum Exporting Countries (OPEC) retaliated against the United States with an oil embargo. OPEC was trying to help its fellow Arabs, but it was also making a point about economics. In the early 1950s, most oil used by Americans came from American oil wells. By 1973, the Middle East was supplying a great deal of the oil that the United States used.

The change in market share resulted from the very low exploration and production costs in the Persian Gulf. Oil is so plentiful in that region that often only cursory exploration effort leads to a gusher. The oil is also relatively close to the surface, so drilling costs are low. Although the region tends to be hot, the environment overall is far easier to work in than some other major oil-producing areas, such as Alaska's North Slope and the North Sea. As a result, the OPEC countries' market share had grown dramatically, until they controlled a major portion of the global oil supply.

Prior to the 1973 war in Israel, the price of a barrel of oil in West Texas had averaged $4.31. By the beginning of 1974, the price had increased to more than $10.

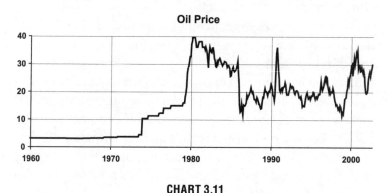

Oil Price

CHART 3.11

The oil price run-up in 1973 illustrates a phenomenon we call a "supply shock." Most of the causes of recession act on the economy by reducing demand for goods and services. However, a recession can also be caused or aggravated by a sudden change in the supply of a key commodity. Most of the significant supply shocks have been oil related, but other kinds of supply shocks are possible.

To understand how oil prices affect a country, imagine a nation that is energy independent. For example, Great Britain currently produces about as much oil from the North Sea as it uses domestically. Even though Britain continues to be self-sufficient in oil, its local oil prices will rise and fall with world prices. From April of 2005 through April of 2006, U.S. gasoline prices excluding taxes rose by 27 percent, causing drivers much grief when they filled up their gas tanks. Was it any better in energy-independent Great Britain? Over the same period, U.K. gas prices excluding taxes rose 29 percent. If they hadn't risen about in line with global prices, oil companies would have moved fuel from locations where it is cheap to locations where it is expensive. That supply shift would have brought prices in the two locations back into line with each other.

Within the energy-independent nation, a rise in oil prices shifts wealth from oil consumers to oil producers. The higher cost of oil has a negative effect on non-oil spending by consumers and businesses. This is offset by the increase in spending by the owners of the oil. The oil price hike merely moves dollars out of one person's pocket and into another person's pocket. For the oil consumers, it's an unfortunate shift. For the oil producers, however, it's great. For the nation, it's no big deal: One person's gain offsets the other's loss. (Along with the change in wealth from oil consumers to oil producers, the oil-producing regions of the country expand at the expense of the oil-consuming regions.)

When we use imported oil, however, the higher price doesn't shift the peas around on our plate; it sends the peas overseas to the oil sheiks. Our country is worse off because we have to send more resources overseas to pay for our imported oil.

Supply shock is the term economists use for the sudden reduction in the availability of a resource. "Suddenness" is important because gradual changes don't cause recessions. We gradually shift our spending to reflect the higher energy tab. We would be better off with lower oil prices, but the effect of a gradual increase is a small reduction in the annual growth rate of the economy, spread over several years.

"Supply shock is the term economists use for the sudden reduction in the availability of a resource."

After sudden oil-price increases, consumers typically continue buying almost as much gas and oil as they had before. There will be some reduction in energy usage, but it is hard to change consumption patterns in the short run. Given enough time, there will be a significant change in consumption, but here we are focusing on short-run effects. Energy consumers will spend more on petroleum products in dollar terms, though the quantity of energy they buy, measured in barrels of oil or cubic feet of natural gas, will be slightly less. Consumers thus have less money to spend on other goods. That "less to spend on other goods" is the trigger for a recession, which will be followed by the inventory draw down and capital spending slump that is typical of recessions.

The oil-price increases tend to push up inflation. This occurs directly as the energy component of the Consumer

Price Index (and other measures of inflation) increase rapidly. There is also an indirect inflation effect. Businesses experience higher costs, both to manufacture their products and to transport them to the customers. At least some of the cost increase is passed on to consumers through higher prices. This ripple effect reinforces the direct increase in inflation caused by the higher oil prices.

Monetary policy is more challenging in these circumstances. The oil-price increase tends to raise prices and depress the economy. It is far more common for the Fed to have to fight only one of these problems at a time than to have to face both at once. The Fed can help to keep the economy going by rapidly easing, pulling down interest rates to give the economy a shot in the arm. The higher oil prices, though, in an economy with stable production, will push the general price level up. Then inflation worsens.

In the twelve months leading up to the Arab oil embargo, inflation had risen dramatically. The growth rate of the Consumer Price Index rose from 3.2 percent to 7.4 percent. The idea of letting inflation continue to roar out of control was not pleasant.

The alternative open to the Fed, however, was possibly worse: tighten monetary policy to limit inflation. However, higher interest rates would further aggravate the recession prompted by the oil-price hike.

The Fed can also split the difference, leaving us with some extra inflation and a little recession, which we call "stagflation."

In addition to the 1973 oil embargo described above, a major disruption in 1979 associated with the Iran hostage crisis caused oil prices to jump from $15 a barrel to nearly $40 a barrel. An American recession followed almost immediately, though we cannot blame the recession solely on the oil shock. The greater cause was monetary policy. The Fed had decided to get tough on inflation with severely restrictive monetary policy. Interest rates jumped sharply, with the Fed Funds rate moving from 10 percent in early 1979 to over 17 percent in the spring of 1980. That was certainly enough to cause a recession without an oil shock. However, the jump in oil prices might have also been enough to cause the recession. The double whammy made the early 1980s one of the worst periods ever for our economy.

If you're a business manager who is trying to assess economic risk, simply watching oil prices is not a good way to be alert for oil-price shocks. Oil prices are not only causes of economic actions but resultants as well. In the late 1990s, oil prices declined rapidly due to the Asian financial crisis. Demand for oil fell as Asian economic activity declined. Falling demand for oil led quite naturally to falling oil prices. Yet rather than a positive oil shock associated with a subsequent boom, this was instead the result of a weakening economy. The eventual rebound in industrial production around the world was accompanied by higher oil prices. This rise in oil prices was not a supply shock, but a demand-driven price reaction. So oil-price watchers need to consider if the rise in oil price is due to supply or demand. If it's demand, then it's not likely to trigger a recession. If it's supply, though, it could be indicative of a supply shock.

From the business manager's perspective, the key questions are these:

1. Is a supply shock occurring?
2. Is it severe enough to significantly affect the economy?
3. What will be the result of the shock?

Small supply shocks occur frequently. Like small earthquakes in California, they become part of the background, with little consequence for the most part.

Supply shocks are not limited to oil. A major strike in the steel industry was a contributing factor in the 1960 recession. The strike depressed consumer spending because the striking workers had no income. More significantly, the strike disrupted the flow of steel through the manufacturing sector of the economy, disrupting production and employment in a number of important industries, such as automobiles and home appliances.

Poor crop harvests, which caused rising food prices, were part of the run-up to the 1973–1975 recession and constituted a minor supply shock.

One researcher found evidence of an oil-price increase behind every post-war recession in the United States. It would be overreaching to say that every recession was caused by a supply shock, however. For one thing, booms tend to pull commodity prices up, which the Federal Reserve takes as an indicator of future inflation. If a recession follows the Fed's action, the cause was not the rise in commodity prices; rather, it was overreaction to the boom that caused the high commodity prices. Furthermore, there have been many supply shocks not followed by recessions. The reasonable position is probably that some supply shocks have tipped the balance in an already-weak economy. Thus, understanding the combinations of factors at work is important.

It's pretty safe to ignore most supply changes, except for major oil price disruptions. However, the future doesn't always look like the past, and there's certainly the possibility of a new kind of supply shock arising. In general, you are better off as a business manager if you consider the day's news to be unimportant and don't fear the continual doom and gloom that newspapers make their money selling.

When we are in the midst of a supply shock, one critical issue is how the Fed will respond. If the Fed holds the line on monetary policy, then dig in for a recession. If the Fed eases aggressively, don't worry about the recession, but instead anticipate severe price increases as inflation heats up. If the Fed seems to be picking a middle ground, then look for both recession and a run-up in prices.

KEY POINTS

Supply shocks primarily consist of oil-price increases but can include other goods, such as steel.	Supply shocks are a secondary cause of recession, adding difficulty when the economy is otherwise weak.

OTHER RECESSIONARY FACTORS

The other factors behind recession are usually not enough to fully trigger a recession by themselves. They may be contributing factors, but there is little evidence that in the American economy any of these will ever be strong enough to cause a recession without either a monetary contraction or possibly a supply shock. Nonetheless, these factors can cause a slowdown in the economy's growth rate. They can also tip a slow-growing economy over the edge. By themselves, though, they are not worth much worry.

Credit Crunches

When loans are available at a high interest rate, we say that monetary policy is tight. When loans are unavailable, regardless of the interest rate that a borrower is willing to pay, we say there is a credit crunch.

The classic credit crunches occurred in the 1960s and 1970s, when banks and savings-and-loans were limited in the interest that they could pay to depositors. When market interest rates rose above these limits, then large depositors would cash in their certificates of deposit (CDs) from banks and thrifts and buy commercial paper or treasury bills, which had unregulated interest rates. This hurt those institutions, which were especially dependent on CDs. When the CDs were cashed in for securities with higher interest rates out-side the bank and thrift industry, the thrifts had no funds available to make new loans. New lending came to a complete standstill. Higher interest rates on loans could not solve the problem because banks could not use higher interest income to pay higher interest rates on deposits. The banks and thrifts had to resort to "non-price rationing" of credit, meaning that they simply did not meet the underlying demand for credit.

Deregulation of interest rates on deposits has prevented such credit crunches from recurring, but other types of crunches are possible. In the early 1990s, for example, bank lending fell dramatically even though the banks had plenty of funds available. However, the banks had been making large loans on commercial real estate, many of which turned sour. Not only did some banks lose their appetite for real estate lending, bank regulators also severely tightened their policies toward real estate lending. Bank examiners were ordering large write-offs of real estate loans. That didn't mean that the loans were forgiven, just that the banks had to file financial statements as if the loans were uncollectible.

Plenty of strange business behavior occurred in this envi-ronment. Some borrowers who had never missed a loan payment were told that their bank wanted to end the loan ahead of schedule. Because the bank had no legal grounds to demand early payment, they offered an incentive: pay us 90 percent of the loan balance remaining now, and we'll forgive the other 10 percent. After borrowers got over the insult implicit in such an offer, they scrambled to find funding to take advantage of the deals. In this era, obviously, few new loans were made for commercial real estate construction.

In the years following the crunch, some banks reported negative loan losses. That means that recoveries on loans that the banks had previously written off exceeded current defaults. Negative loan losses result from very good luck today or overly extreme write-offs yesterday. In practice, the write-offs of the early 1990s were extreme to the point of absurdity.

The characteristic of a credit crunch is some dramatic change in the environment, which prevents banks (or other lenders) from doing business as they previously had. There is a normal tightening of credit standards in a recession, but we don't call this a crunch. There is always difficulty for companies that are bad credit risks who want or need to borrow. We don't call this a credit crunch, either.

> **"The characteristic of a credit crunch is some dramatic change in the environment, which prevents banks (or other lenders) from doing business as they previously had."**

The Asian financial crisis, discussed in more detail in Chapter 8, included elements of a credit crunch. Credit might have been available to a borrower willing to pay a high enough interest rate, but the crisis disrupted normal relationships among borrowers and lenders. Until new relationships could be built, credit stopped flowing.

At this time, the prospects of another credit crunch in the United States appear slim. Reports of banks tightening credit are normal in recessions and should not be taken as indicating anything other than a typical downturn. But the business manager should be aware of the possibility of changes in regulations that suddenly limit lenders' ability to meet the credit needs of their usual customers. In Chapter 8, which covers foreign business cycles, we'll give more attention to problems caused by credit crunches in some other countries.

Waves of Optimism and Pessimism

John Maynard Keynes thought that psychological factors were important causes behind recessions. He particularly expected business investment to be quite volatile, for psychological reasons. He noted that much business decision-making is based on fairly weak fundamentals.

A small excursion into theory will help the business manager understand the basis for important decisions. Keynes implicitly drew upon a distinction developed by the American economist Frank Knight between risk and uncertainty. If someone shows you a standard deck of cards, and proposes a bet on a red jack being drawn, it is fairly easy for you to calculate the probability. Two red jacks among fifty-two cards means a probability of two in fifty-two, or about 4 percent. Whether or not you bet depends on the payoff, your resources, and your attitude toward risk. The decision should not be hard to make.

But suppose, instead, you are presented with a deck of 100 round cards, and asked if you want to bet on a blue turtle being drawn from the deck. You have no idea how many turtles of any color would be in this strange deck, much less how many of them would be blue. You are totally ignorant about the odds. The first bet is a case of risk, because the probability of a red jack is known. The second bet is a case of uncertainty, because we don't have any clue what the probability of a blue turtle is.

Some business decisions are based on fairly well-understood probabilities. Should we replace that boiler? An engineer might estimate a 5 percent chance the old one will fail in the coming year. The cost of a failure can be calculated and compared to cost of a new boiler. These decisions have a fairly sound basis. Although we never really know the odds with perfect precision, we usually get in the ballpark. This is an example of risk.

Some business decisions, however, are "blue turtles." Keynes emphasized the business decisions based on uncertainty. He said that we have no idea what the probabilities are regarding the price of copper twenty years from now or interest rates twenty years from now. Given such uncertainty, decisions made today regarding such things—should we build a new copper smelter—will have a very squishy underpinning. A bit more optimism across the business community leads to many new projects. A bit more pessimism leads to a large reduction in capital spending.

Keynes developed this idea of moodiness at the business level into economy-wide swings between optimism and pessimism. He noted that in matters of uncertainty, business managers tend to follow the crowd. If one person is uncertain about what to do, he or she takes a cue from what other managers are doing. If they are all, for instance, buying new information technology systems to engage in electronic commerce, then the uncertain manager will also feel inclined to buy a new IT system. Even without knowledge of the probability of new revenue or reduced cost, the manager follows the crowd. There is comfort and security in doing what one's peers are doing.

As Brad DeLong of the University of California has recently observed, technological change increases uncertainty. Twenty years ago, a CEO might have asked how much it would cost to change accounting systems and what the benefits would be. The operations chief could have estimated the cost of clerks and their mechanical adding machines, desks, and so on. The cost of the computer alternative was also fairly well known, so the CEO could get pretty accurate estimates.

However, in 2000 the information technology chief would have had a harder time quantifying the benefits of a new accounting system. The new system might be critical in interfacing with Web-based transactions, in mining customer transactions for further sales leads, and for interfacing with a production planning system. But how important will these features be in the near future? No one really knew in 2000, so the company was facing uncertainty, not risk.

With most business managers doing whatever the other managers are doing, we have lots of business managers who move all together to increase their capital spending at the same time or to reduce their capital spending at the same time. The result, Keynes believed, is a tendency toward business cycles.

However, we should not interpret this to mean that our business and political leaders have much influence over attitudes. We sometimes hear that "we can talk ourselves into" recession. In my experience, none of our leaders is influential enough to noticeably change popular perception. I first attempted an economic forecast as a high school student in early 1970. I remember picking up the newspaper to see a bold headline: "Nixon Says Economy Healthy." I decided that if the president *needs* to proclaim that the economy is healthy, then there was probably a problem. In fact, the economy was already in recession by the time Nixon was asked about it.

If you are managing a business, it does make sense for you to pay attention to what other people are thinking. That's not to be a slave to fashion but rather to be an observer of attitudes. Ignore the president, ignore the corporate CEO on the cover of *Fortune*, ignore the columnists. Also ignore the farmers (who always say that times are hard), and ignore the retail merchants (who will tell you that business is great right up to their "going out of business" sale). Instead, listen to the everyday business managers, both mid-level and senior-level executives. When those who had once been optimistic start sounding gloomy, it's time to get nervous.

Consumer Confidence

If psychology can affect business decisions, it should certainly be able to influence consumer decisions. Most variation in consumer attitudes, though, is fairly predictable: People have high confidence when they are employed and when inflation is low. This basic calculation, however, goes awry during unusual times, such as during the buildup of troops in the Middle East prior to the Persian Gulf War of 1990–1991.

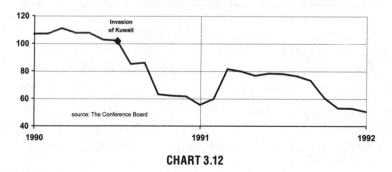

Consumer Confidence

CHART 3.12

Waves of optimism or pessimism can affect spending, though not nearly as much as the fundamentals do. Generally, it's a good bet that consumers will spend most of what they earn. Unusual circumstances, however, can alter the percentage spent in either direction. The drop in consumer confidence in the build-up to the Gulf War did depress consumer spending. However, the drop in confidence following the September 11 terrorist attacks did not affect spending significantly. Recall that in the wake of the attacks, automobile manufacturers offered zero percent financing on new cars and trucks, and the Fed cut interest rates. The conclusion we reach is that confidence should usually be ignored in favor of fundamentals. When there is a major noneconomic event that impacts confidence, then the survey reports should be considered carefully.

Don't expect political leaders to have a great impact on consumer behavior. The opinion leaders who are reported in the press may sway attitudes, but that's not enough. For there

BUSINOMICS SURVEYS OF CONSUMER ATTITUDES

▶ There are two major surveys of consumer attitudes, the Survey of Consumer Confidence by the Conference Board, and the Survey of Consumer Sentiment by the University of Michigan's Survey Research Center. Both ask questions of a sample of households every month. Questions include whether jobs are easy to find and whether it's a good time to buy a major appliance. The questions are about both current conditions and expectations for the future. The two surveys differ in the specific questions asked and in the survey method, so they don't always track one another, but they generally tell the same story.

to be an economic effect, actual spending must be changed. When the fundamentals of strong consumer-income growth and low inflation are in place, there's nothing a leader can do to stop people from buying. And when the underlying economic conditions have gone south, there is nothing the president can say that will get people to go shopping.

Fiscal Policy

Sharp fluctuations in government activity can be recessionary—but don't overdramatize this effect. We can have a perfectly healthy economy with a small government. However, the transition from a large government sector to a small government sector can be difficult. The United States was hit by recession in 1945 as the European war effort wound down but before the war in the Pacific was over. Surprisingly to many Keynesians who looked to government spending to be the dominant factor in business cycles, no recession materialized in 1946 or 1947 as the war effort was finally over and government spending fell sharply. Pent-up consumer demand replaced government spending in the years immediately following World War II.

The 1970 recession is often attributed, at least in part, to the winding down of the Vietnam War. Defense spending (inflation adjusted) hit its peak in mid-1968, then declined gradually for two years, with the most rapid decline occurring in the first half of 1970, in the midst of recession. However, the decline in military expenditures wasn't the only thing going on. In the twelve months leading up to the economy's peak, the Fed tightened monetary policy. The growth rate of the money supply dropped sharply, from 8.0 percent to 3.7 percent growth, and the Fed Funds rate shot up from

6 percent to 9 percent. The role of the defense cutback in 1970 was contributory, but not decisive, in causing the recession.

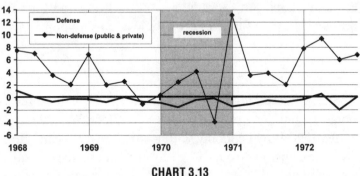

Contributions to Real GDP Change

CHART 3.13

Most changes in government spending are more gradual than these military-driven changes. They generate their largest effects in the press, but relatively minor effects on business. The people most affected—and their representatives in Congress—talk as if government spending is the mother's milk of the economy, but the reality is that most changes in government spending are of no great significance to business. The obvious exceptions are businesses selling to the government. To these firms, monitoring the political scene is a basic part of their economic early warning system.

Fiscal policy is often given large attention because it is easily seen. New aircraft carriers are built, highways are constructed, federal buildings are opened. The "unseen" offsets, however, are also pretty strong. (I'm borrowing language on the "seen" and the "unseen" from French economist Frederic Bastiat.) If taxes are used to finance the spending, then taxpayers have less disposable income. Their spending will be lower than it otherwise would have been. If deficit finance is used, then lenders will divert their funds away from private lending into government bonds. There will be less money available for private investment, and we say that the government spending has "crowded out" private capital spending.

However, a ramp-up in federal expenditures can probably accelerate the spending of money, so there is a temporary surge for one or possibly two quarters, after which the effects will be reversed. In other words, the federal government gets the money spent sooner than the taxpayer would have spent his own money. An economist focusing on predicting gross domestic product over the next quarter or two should look carefully at changes in government spending. The business manager looking out four quarters or more, however, can safely say that the effects of government spending will wash out over that time period. The exception would be strong, rapid, and continuing increases in government spending. Even then, look for a reversal of the stimulating effects once government spending stops accelerating, as it inevitably must.

Foreign Business Cycles

International events can also be contributing factors to domestic recession. First, global recessions can certainly hit the United States. The world is becoming more synchronized, with greater trade flows, so it is quite reasonable to see more impact from foreign recessions on the United States. The trade data support the hypothesis of increased globalization. The total volume of trade (imports *plus* exports) has grown at twice the economy's overall growth rate in recent decades, indicating that the countries of the world are more economically connected than ever before. However, it's hard to identify any modern U.S. recession triggered by foreign recession.

For example, Japan's recession—or, some would say, depression—proceeded for quite some time while the U.S. economy was booming. Japan is such a large economy, and such a large trading partner to the United States, that if anyone's recession were going to hurt us, it should have been Japan's. But we escaped unscathed.

Real GDP Growth: U.S. and Japan

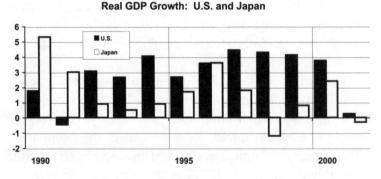

CHART 3.14

The Asian financial crisis of 1997–1998 slowed U.S. exports, but it hardly put a dent in our economy. There was a slowdown in sectors of our economy that export heavily to the Far East, and in a few states that are dependent on that trade, but no general economic slowdown. Probably the greatest problem was with nonresidential construction, some of which was dependent on high-risk debt. Lenders lost their taste for risky debt during the crisis, causing some construction projects to be postponed or cancelled.

Trade Wars

Restrictions on foreign trade can be recessionary, with the Great Depression providing a good example. Early in 1929, the U.S. Congress considered legislation to dramatically increase our tariffs. The Smoot-Hawley tariff was recognized by business as likely to reduce U.S. imports dramatically. Even worse, the tariff was likely to cause retaliation by other countries, so our exports would decline if Congress adopted the tariff. Some economists consider the tariff to be a cause of the stock market crash, as investors recognized how bad the tariff would be for business. No one would seriously claim this foreign trade dispute as the major cause of the long-lasting depression. However, it certainly was an additional factor behind the downturn.

Speculative Manias

Investment bubbles can lead to a boom in spending, followed by a crash. The Japanese real estate boom of the 1980s contributed to that country's depression in the 1990s. The American high-tech and telecom stock market bubble was followed by the recession of 2001. Other manias include the South Sea bubble of the 1600s and railroad stocks in the early 1800s.

The great tulip craze of Holland in 1636–1637 illustrates how it works. People see rising prices for some commodity, such as tulip bulbs. They purchase bulbs on speculation, and watch the prices rise. The price of some tulip bulbs rose as high as $2,000 and even $4,000 per bulb in terms of today's prices. It may seem that the bubble would be self-limiting, as buyers have to raise cash to buy bulbs, and this need for cash will limit the boom. But most owners of bulbs can just sit back and watch a few people buy and sell in the market. The owners recalculate their own net worth as they see the small number of sales occur at rising prices. With greater wealth in their bulb holdings, people start spending more. First they may spend all of their income, leaving nothing to add to savings. Their logic is that their bulb investment has risen in value as much as they had wanted to save. Second, people may start liquidating other investments, either in bulbs or in other assets, to fund their spending. This higher level of spending seems justified by their new level of wealth.

Eventually, however, economic fundamentals will come into play. More bulbs can be produced, albeit somewhat slowly. (In the case of real estate, more buildings can be built. In the case of technology stocks, more companies will be formed and go public.) The price of the asset will be limited by the cost of creating new products. A few investors will catch on to this and start to take their profits. As prices begin to fall, more and more investors try to sell to lock in their profits, but few buyers will appear. Prices will continue to edge down, then the price decline will accelerate and prices will fall sharply.

People who had been spending aggressively will reevaluate their standard of living in light of their new, lower level of wealth. Consumer spending will drop drastically if the bubble was rooted in household behavior.

If the bubble was in real estate, there will be a cessation of new construction, throwing that industry into recession. The construction recession will be compounded by a cutback in spending by the owners of the real estate.

If the bubble was in stocks, the cutback will be in new business formations and in the spending by owners of stock.

The economist Charles Kindleberger studied speculative manias and bubbles extensively, and he concluded that there is an element of monetary overexpansion behind most of them. That is, the Federal Reserve or other central bank made too much money available to the economy, fueling the fire of speculation. The eventual slowing of money-supply growth prevents the bubble from continuing indefinitely. Thus, even the bubble is a companion cause of recession, rather than a prime mover in and of itself.

KEY POINT

A wide variety of factors can hurt the economy.
Most are not strong enough, in itself, to cause a recession,
but several added together can trigger a downturn.

SUMMING UP

There will always be something wrong with the economy, but usually the problems do not trigger recession. The discussion of causes of recession may lead the business manager to experience something akin to "medical student syndrome," in which students have been found to display symptoms of the diseases they are studying. A large dose of optimism is in order, for most of the time the economy expands. We have taken so much time dealing with recession because that is when businesses often fail or experience serious losses. Like medicine, most of the time an understanding of recessions is of little use, but when it's needed, it's really needed. As we will learn in Chapter 5, thinking about recessions in good times will lay the groundwork for strong defense against an economic slowdown, so long as caution does not overwhelm the manager and lead to extreme reluctance to take risk.

BUSINOMICS

Inflation: Recession Triggers and Profit Squeezes

WILLIAM B. CONERLY, PH.D.—As a young corporate economist in the early 1980s, my forecast presentations always included a lengthy discussion of inflation. Now I often skip the topic entirely. Is inflation less important than we thought a couple of decades ago? Not really. What has changed is that inflation is well under control. As a result, a host of issues that can arise from high inflation rates and volatile inflation rates have become moot. However, good business decisions still require important information about inflation. First, the inflation data show varying rates of change for different goods. Many of these relationships are enduring, so that management can exploit this information for years to come. Second, the Federal Reserve still worries about inflation, and the Fed's worries constitute the primary driver of monetary policy today. Finally, sometimes a company's costs increase much faster than their product prices, squeezing profit margins down to nothing. Foreseeing these inflation changes is crucial to maintaining profitability.

THE FACTS ABOUT INFLATION

Three types of inflation rates are commonly discussed, though there are thousands of specific indexes to choose from. The Consumer Price Index (CPI) is the best known and still useful for many purposes, though generally not the preferred choice of statistical connoisseurs. The Producer Price Index (PPI), formerly known as the Wholesale Price Index, covers goods sold by manufacturers, farmers, and wholesalers. Finally, measures of wage inflation are important because so much of a typical business's costs are labor-related.

However, the big picture of inflation can be viewed with the most common indexes, even though none of them is really perfect. A more specific analysis of a business problem should involve careful attention to the correct index. For now, let's look at some data rather than nitpicking the details.

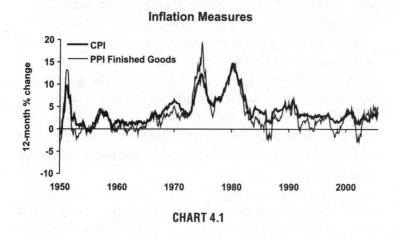

CHART 4.1

Goods prices are more volatile than total consumer prices. Chart 4.1 compares the CPI to the PPI in terms of twelve-month percentage changes. Notice that the CPI line is relatively more stable. The highest peaks and the lowest troughs come from the PPI, not the CPI. There are also more wiggles from year to year in the PPI than the CPI, especially in the 1980s and 1990s. Our first conclusion, then, is that consumer prices are more stable than producer prices. This conclusion about price corresponds to the conclusion about sales volumes from the last chapter: Consumer sales are more stable than wholesale sales.

Consumer prices tend to rise faster than goods prices. Compare the average level of the two indexes. In general, the CPI is as high, or higher, than the PPI. The exceptions tend to be those times when the PPI is spiking upward. Our second conclusion, then, is that consumer price inflation averages higher than producer price inflation. Backing up this conclusion, the long-run growth rate of the CPI is 3.7 percent per year, but PPI has grown by 3.0 percent per year. That's not a huge difference, but it does compound over time.

Both the CPI and the PPI have many subcomponents, as well as aggregates that include "everything but," such as "all items except food and energy." The components of the major price indexes show variations that are critical to businesses buying or selling this stuff. (Pure service businesses may skip over the next few paragraphs, unless they are providing services to a firm that handles goods at the manufacturer or wholesale level.)

One point worth repeating is that the subcomponent for commodities within the CPI grows at a significantly slower rate than the index for services: 3.4 percent annual average for goods, compared to 5.0 percent for services.

As a general rule, raw materials have more volatile pricing than finished goods, with intermediate goods (some processing has occurred, but more is needed) in the middle. Thus, wheat prices have great volatility; flour prices are somewhat more stable; and bread prices are the most stable of them all. This same pattern would also apply to metals, petroleum, and other materials, but let's stick with the wheat example for a minute.

The price of wheat spiked up in early 1992, rising 59 percent in twelve months' time. Flour prices rose 29 percent, but bread only rose 3 percent. The overall CPI rose less than 3 percent during this period. Six months later, the price of bread was up 7 percent, showing the time lags involved. So the rise in the price of wheat pushed up the price of flour and had a small impact on the price of bread. A similar pattern emerged when wheat prices fell sharply in 1997. Wheat dropped by 34 percent, while flour dropped 24 percent. Bread prices rose over 2 percent, roughly in line with overall consumer inflation.

> **"The important point for business leaders to know is that crude materials prices are highly volatile, but they have low average-growth rates."**

The important point for business leaders to know is that crude materials prices are highly volatile, but they have low average-growth rates. Agricultural products, crude oil, and steel scrap all have wild price fluctuations on a regular basis. The price swings of processed foods, cold-rolled steel, and diesel fuel are a little milder, but they are still far greater than the price changes that consumers experience.

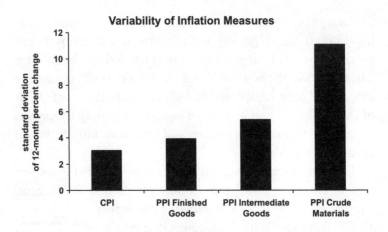

CHART 4.2

Consumer Price Index (CPI): All goods and services typically bought by urban consumers. Examples include bread in the supermarket for sale to consumers; the rental value of your home; health care services.

Producer Price Index, Finished Goods: Goods sold by manufacturers or wholesalers that are ready for the end user. An example is bread sold by wholesaler to the supermarket. No services.

Producer Price Index, Intermediate Goods: Goods that have been processed, but will need further processing. Examples include wheat flour, thread, lumber. No services.

Producer Price Index, Crude Materials: Materials that have not been processed at all. Examples include wheat, crude oil, iron ore.

In addition to differences in volatility, the various inflation measures have different trend growth rates.

TABLE 4-A

	Long-Run Growth Rate, %
Consumer Price Index	3.7
Producer Price Index:	
Finished goods	3.0
Intermediate goods	3.2
Crude materials	2.7
Employee Compensation	5.4

Labor costs are responsible for the higher trend growth of the Consumer Price Index. The world's manufacturers and farmers have become tremendously more efficient. The amount of labor needed to make a motor or to grow a bushel of wheat is far, far less than in years past.

However, service-sector efficiency has not improved commensurately. My barber takes about as long to cut my hair now as he did twenty years ago, despite some recession of my hairline. In an example often used by economists, it has been 200 years since Beethoven wrote his string quartets. In that time, there has been no reduction in the number of musicians needed to play a string quartet, nor has there been any reduction in the amount of time it takes to play a string quartet. In other words, no productivity improvement at all.

As a result, the cost of having a string quartet perform has risen tremendously relative to the cost of growing a bushel of wheat or of producing a cotton gin.

Because different price indexes have different rates of change, there is no one inflation rate. When Federal Reserve officials state that they are targeting a stable inflation rate, it's not immediately obvious whether they want commodity prices to be stable or consumer prices to be stable. Here's a critically important point for understanding the Fed's work: *It's generally impossible to get both consumer prices and commodity prices stable at the same time.* If consumer prices are not changing, then commodity prices are probably falling. If commodity prices are stable, then consumer prices are probably rising. We'll return to this issue below.

Business leaders should expect that their labor-intensive processes will become more expensive at a faster rate than their less-labor-intensive processes. However, that said, those labor-intensive processes will not fluctuate as much as their materials cost.

KEY POINTS			
Price inflation for services is more stable than for goods.	Price inflation for services is higher, on average, than for goods.	Crude materials prices are more volatile than finished goods prices.	Labor costs inflation is more stable than other goods and services inflation, but it has a higher trend growth rate.

INFLATION AND FEDERAL RESERVE POLICY

Fighting inflation is a key motivation for Federal Reserve tightening. Understanding the Fed's thinking about inflation is necessary for understanding when they will raise interest rates to cool down economic growth. The challenge for the business leader appears substantial: Follow the attitudes of the twelve key decision-makers on the Federal Open Market Committee, even though the membership of the committee turns over regularly. Actually, it's much, much easier than it sounds. The Federal Reserve now has a stable, consistent view of how it should respond to inflation. Their skill at implementing monetary policy will vary with the membership, but their overall approach will remain the same for years to come. To understand why, let's explore a bit of the history of economic thought.

The Phillips Curve dominated thinking about inflation in the 1960s. The economist A. W. H. Phillips published a paper in 1958 studying the relationship between unemployment and inflation in the United Kingdom since 1861. He found a pronounced inverse correlation. Phillips did not postulate a theory to go with the data, but the implication of his curve was obvious: If we want low inflation, we have to tolerate high unemployment. If we want low unemployment, we have to tolerate high inflation. American data seemed to support Phillips, as shown by Chart 4.3.

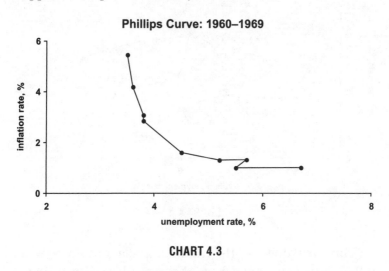

Phillips Curve: 1960–1969

CHART 4.3

Economists thought that macroeconomic policy simply boiled down to assessing the relative harm done by unemployment, compared to the harm done by inflation. Not surprisingly, unemployment seemed to be the greater evil.

While the theorists worked out the logic in the connection between the two variables, policymakers drove unemployment down with easy money, as well as fiscal stimulus. Lyndon Johnson inaugurated his Great Society social programs while stepping up the war in Vietnam. The Fed kept interest rates low, willing to accept higher inflation in order to keep unemployment low.

Unfortunately, the Phillips Curve broke down as policymakers began to use it. The decade of the 1970s showed increasing unemployment *and* inflation; as mentioned earlier, this is a pattern dubbed "stagflation."

Phillips Curve: 1969–1980

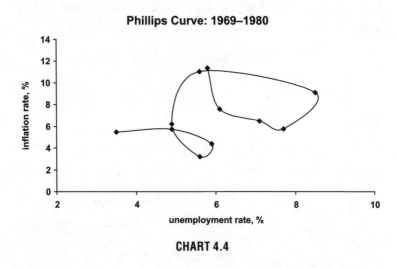

CHART 4.4

This breakdown in the traditional relationship between inflation and unemployment theory had been anticipated by two economists. Milton Friedman and Edmund Phelps, both of whom would later win Nobel Prizes, independently developed the following idea: In the long run, there is no tradeoff between unemployment and inflation. However, in the short-run, there is a tradeoff between unemployment and *unanticipated* inflation. The Federal Reserve can reduce unemployment by surprising people with unanticipated inflation. However, people will try to anticipate inflation so as not to be fooled. Their anticipation of inflation makes it harder and harder to reduce unemployment. Either the Fed gives up the fight against unemployment to rein in inflation, or inflation goes to hyper-inflation rates, eventually leading to a severe recession to bring it back down.

Long-Term Growth and Inflation

Long-term growth and inflation form the next piece of the puzzle. Even if there is no short-run tradeoff between inflation and unemployment, there does seem to be a long-term *cost* to high inflation. Countries with high inflation rates tend to have volatile inflation rates. This volatility makes business planning difficult. A banker is hesitant to lend money for a long period of time if he's not sure what inflation is going to be. A business owner is hesitant to build a factory and commit to selling you goods for a certain price if he doesn't know what inflation is going to be. These decisions accumulate when inflation is unstable, leading to a slower rate of growth. In fact, when Alan Greenspan was asked to define what he meant by low inflation, he replied that he wanted inflation to not be a factor in business decisions.

The new economic theory has two clear conclusions:

1. The Federal Reserve cannot reduce unemployment, except temporarily.
2. Low inflation is preferable to high inflation.

The implication of these two points is that the best policy simply keeps inflation low.

There are certainly difficulties in implementing this policy. Time lags between cause and effect make it hard for the Fed to know what to do at any particular moment. Various forces and nonquantifiable factors, such as consumer attitudes and geopolitical risks, have to be considered. Regardless of the practical difficulties, though, look for the Federal Reserve to continue its efforts to keep inflation low, so low that it is not a factor in business decisions.

KEY POINTS

There is no long-term tradeoff between inflation and unemployment that policymakers can exploit to reduce unemployment.	The Federal Reserve now has a stable policy: *Keep inflation low.*

BUSINESS DECISIONS AND PROFIT SQUEEZES

Businesses face two types of risks related to pricing cycles. One is an industry cycle in which overinvestment in productive capacity leads to low prices for finished products. This is discussed in Chapter 10. The other risk is the subject of this section: costs of raw materials rising faster than the prices of finished products.

The global economic boom of 2004–2005 provides ample illustrations of rising costs for industrial materials. I give many speeches every year, and I can usually tell what's on business leaders' minds by the questions they ask. In this time period, I was suddenly inundated by questions about rising costs. For example, in one audience I spotted a woman whose face seemed troubled when I mentioned inflation. She ran a specialty nut-and-bolt manufacturing company, she said, and she wanted to know if she would see relief on steel prices. At another speech, the owner of a heavy construction company told me about stiffly rising costs of cement, as well as steel. When I spoke to the nurserymen's association, I heard about the cost of shipping trees and shrubs as diesel fuel prices hit new highs. Yet in this period, consumer price inflation remained fairly restrained. Nonfuel inflation rates stayed well below 3 percent. However, companies that purchased large amounts of steel, cement, or fuel and that could not increase the prices of their finished products were caught in a profit squeeze. The worst losers had bid on large projects on a fixed-cost basis, without locking in their materials costs.

Coping with this risk begins with understanding the volatility of prices of the company's key raw materials. For some materials, industry sources or futures markets provide good data on prices. Current and historical price data are available for most fuel and metals. Many other materials prices are also easy to obtain. For materials not readily available, look for the Producer Price Index that comes closest. (Links to a number of government statistics are available at *www.businomics.com.*)

As a general rule, materials that have been processed more have more stable prices. Consider gasoline. As a consumer, you pay a price that must, on average, cover the cost of crude oil, of refining crude into gasoline, of transporting the fuel to your local gas station, and of operating the gas station. The price also includes taxes, most often figured on a cents-per-gallon rather than a percentage basis. If the supply of oil is disrupted and the price of crude oil rises, most of those other costs and taxes do not rise.

Similarly, if global demand for energy is pulling up crude oil prices, most of the other costs will not be rising. The only case in which gasoline would rise by as much or more than crude oil is if demand in your local market area rose rapidly, allowing retailers and distributors to increase their profit margins (until new entrants could enter the market and bring profit margins back down).

After examining historical data to assess the company's vulnerability to rising costs, the next step is to establish an early warning system to alert the company to rising costs. This price component should be integrated into the early warning system discussed in Chapter 6. The key is to look for two elements: prices of the raw materials used to produce your purchased inputs, and capacity constraints in the production of that input. For example, let's say that you are running a paint company. One of your key costs is for the pigment titanium dioxide, which can contribute as much as 30 percent of the total cost of a bucket of paint. Watching the price of titanium dioxide makes sense. In addition to studying the pigment's prices directly, the company should watch the price of titanium and capacity within the titanium dioxide industry. Titanium has a variety of uses, including golf club heads and underwires in bras, but titanium dioxide is by far the largest use of the element. Watching the price of titanium or titanium ore may indicate incipient price increases in titanium oxide. Check with your vendor to understand just what raw materials prices give the best indication of changes in the vendor's cost structure.

The second factor is capacity utilization within the titanium dioxide processing industry. When actual production nears the industry's capacity, price increases are likely. When clients ask for my help regarding passing on cost increases, one of the key elements we discuss is the level of excess capacity in the industry. If there are plenty of underutilized factories producing the product, users have choices, so price increases probably won't stick. But when all of the producers are making as much of the product as they can, customers who object to a price increase will be left without product.

Thus, the paint manufacturer's early warning system should have on it the actual pigment price, the price of either titanium or titanium dioxide, and the level of capacity utilization within that industry.

The risk a company faces from rising prices depends critically on whether it can pass those higher costs on to its customers. When my clients ask for advice about passing on cost increases, I offer them three criteria. It's easier to pass on cost increases when the following is true:

1. Competitors are facing the same cost increases.
2. The industry has little excess capacity.
3. Your customers can, in turn, pass the cost increases along to their customers.

In most industries, competitors have similar cost structures, so the first condition above will be met. However, if you are making a product out of plastic, whereas many of your competitors are using wood, then you may not be able to pass on plastics cost increases.

BUSINOMICS JARGON MADE CLEAR: *CAPACITY UTILIZATION*

▶ Capacity utilization would be 100 percent if all factories, mines, and utilities were running flat out at all times. Any downtime for maintenance or repair reduces capacity utilization, so 100 percent utilization isn't really feasible. As a result, it's best to look at the figures relative to their historic highs, lows, and average. For instance, capacity utilization in computer and electronic product manufacturing averages about 77 percent. The maximum utilization was 87 percent, at the peak of the tech boom. For this sector, utilization over 80 percent should present red flags; 83 percent is a double red flag.

You can find links to the source data at *www.businomics.com.*

The second condition, regarding industry capacity, may sometimes fool managers in the turnaround after a recession. People get used to conditions and are sometimes slow to recognize changes. A number of companies have acted like a recession was continuing long after capacity utilization was on the upswing. The moral, then, is to use the early-warning system as a guide to raising prices. Finally, the question of whether your customers can pass cost increases along assumes a business-to-business environment. If your customers will have to eat any price increases you make, then you have to make sure that they will be able to continue in business. It does no good to have a higher price list with no customers.

KEY POINTS

Businesses need to assess the price volatility of their key raw materials.	For materials subject to large price variability, an early warning system should monitor price conditions.	Price increases can be passed on to customers when competitors face the same cost increases, when industry excess capacity is low, and when customers will be able to pass cost increases further down the line.

INFLATION CLAUSES IN LONG-TERM CONTRACTS

Long-term contracts often contain price adjustment clauses based on inflation measures. This is a good practice, in general. A contract should benefit both parties. I want beer, and I feel that I'm better off with beer than with money. My local tavern-keeper would rather have money than beer. When we enter into a deal, both of us are better off.

Over a long time period, however, it's hard to know what price will make both of us better off than without any deal. Suppose I'm leasing space for a store. After five years, if inflation has pushed the price tags of my merchandise up by 15 percent, then I can probably afford 15 percent higher rent. Or, if inflation has doubled my price tags, then I can afford to pay twice the rent. But nobody is sure ahead of time what inflation will be, so it's hard to write a contract that will leave everyone happy in the future. The solution is to adjust rents for inflation, or to have the rent consist of a smaller fixed rent plus a percentage of sales.

Inflation adjustments are commonly found in long-term resource contracts. For instance, an electric utility may enter into a long-term agreement with a coal-mining company, with the price to be paid for the coal tied to some measure of inflation, either general or specific to energy prices. The long-term agreement reduces risk to both the buyer and the seller, so long as the inflation adjustment clause is well crafted. Union wage contracts often have a cost-of-living adjustment as well.

Inflation adjustment clauses should be written with the actual government data release specified explicitly. Many times I've been called by someone wanting to know how much inflation has increased, but the specific clause in the contract calls for a version of the Consumer Price Index that does not actually exist, never has existed, and never will exist.

The bigger challenge in writing a long-term inflation adjustment is cost of production versus value of product. Let's take the long-term coal contract mentioned above (which I'm very familiar with, having worked for a coal company with long-term contracts). One approach is to use a measure of inflation in production costs. The mine manager can estimate how much of the total cost of production is from labor, how much diesel fuel for the equipment, how much for wear and tear of the equipment, and so on. A weighted average of various specific inflation measures can approximate changes in production costs. However, that measure will not specifically reflect the value of coal to an electric utility. To do that, one would use a measure of the market price of coal.

One approach makes the mine whole with respect to its costs, but it places upon the coal buyer the risk that production costs rise more than the value of the coal. In fact, that happened in the 1980s. Coal prices fell, and the contracts that looked good in the early 1980s looked awful to the buyers in the late 1980s. However, the alternative, an energy-price adjustment clause, would have hurt the mine: Its costs were rising due to normal inflation, even though the market price of coal was declining.

There is no simple solution. Risk exists and must be allocated between the parties to the contract. However, both parties should strive for contract terms that will be good for both parties over the widest possible range of eventualities. A contract that becomes grossly unfavorable is a contract that will be disputed, at best. At worst, one party may go bankrupt, which does the counterparty no good. My general preference in this situation is to split the difference: half of the price adjustment would be based on cost of production, and half on the value of the coal. This keeps the contract valuable to both parties over a wide range of possible outcomes.

KEY POINTS

Long-term contracts should often include price-adjustment clauses.	Adjustment clauses should be carefully drafted to ensure that both parties benefit over the widest possible range of eventualities.

HOW ACCURATE ARE OUR
MEASURES OF INFLATION?

When newspapers report inflation, invariably someone complains that the Consumer Price Index fails to properly measure living costs. Consumers tend to believe that inflation is higher than the official reports indicate. Economists, on the other hand, tend to believe that the CPI overstates inflation. From the standpoint of business decision-making, the controversy isn't as complicated as it sounds.

The CPI may not accurately measure inflation, but there's no reason to think that we see sharp swings in the error rate. Thus, a rise in inflation from 2 percent to 5 percent may not mean that inflation is truly 5 percent, but it does mean that inflation has increased by about 3 percentage points.

Consumer Price Inflation

CHART 4.5

In Chart 4.5, ignore the little wiggles and focus on the big changes. In 1990, inflation dropped from 6 percent to 3 percent, then in 1997 dropped to nearly 1 percent. These changes are due to actual economic conditions, not measurement errors in the CPI. Thus, the index is useful as an indicator of changes even if it is not perfectly accurate as a measure of consumer prices.

Companies that need an idea of what the Federal Reserve is thinking can look at changes in the CPI and learn enough to understand the big picture. The Fed's economists tend to focus more on a measure called the Price Index for Personal Consumer Expenditures (PCE), and often a variant of this called the Market-Based PCE Index. However, these tend to move up and down with the CPI and don't really have to be monitored by executives already following the CPI.

At other times, a business needs an inflation measure for other purposes, such as to gauge whether its own cost increases are due to inflation or perhaps to lost efficiency. In these circumstances, the CPI is invariably a bad gauge. That's not the fault of the CPI; it's simply that no average index would accurately reflect changes in production costs. Where specific cost increases must be evaluated, the best practice entails creating a weighted average of the most relevant price indexes. It's not hard to do, though it requires some dexterity with data manipulation.

KEY POINTS

The Consumer Price Index is not perfectly accurate, but it does a good job of showing changes in the inflation rate.

For business-analysis purposes, custom-created weighted averages are usually more appropriate.

SUMMING UP

All businesses must be aware of the basic drivers of Federal Reserve policy. The two key elements are these:

- The Fed is committed to low inflation.
- Inflation occurs with a time lag, so the Fed will start fighting inflation when it anticipates inflation, not necessarily when inflation actually increases.

Businesses for whom raw materials constitute a major cost need to be attuned to the volatility of the prices of the things they buy. Those who purchase goods whose prices have historically been very unstable need to manage the business with that volatility in mind. Long-term contracts should take this risk into account. One approach is to hedge by locking in purchase prices the day the contract is signed, assuming that the customer is not going to be able to weasel out of his commitment or go bankrupt if prices fall. Another approach is to have the contract price adjust to the cost of materials. For instance, I commit to build your bridge for a certain price, but that price will be adjusted upward or downward depending on changes in the prices of steel and cement during the construction period. A good attorney can help explore the advantages and disadvantages of different approaches, but the problem cannot be ignored.

Companies that are vulnerable to cost swings due to changes in raw materials prices should put price indicators on their early warning system. Good indicators include the actual costs being paid, the current price of precursor materials, and capacity utilization in the processing industry.

BUSINOMICS

Planning for a Downturn: Vulnerability and Flexibility

WILLIAM B. CONERLY, PH.D.— Every executive or business owner should begin by assessing the business unit's vulnerability to recession. There are a few businesses not susceptible to recession—but *very* few. Most managers who claim that their businesses are not vulnerable to recession are either naïve or less than honest.

In this chapter, we'll focus on the negative: planning for a future downturn or recession. To keep this topic in perspective, remember that the economy spends most of its time expanding and just a little time contracting. Nonetheless, a focus on the negative is necessary because recessions raise the risk of bankruptcy. Less severe financial distress won't cause bankruptcy, but it will limit the company's growth prospects for several years.

On a positive note, many of the techniques that we discuss for dealing with recession would also apply to contingency planning for a boom. Planning for growth is discussed in Chapter 7, but it would make sense for a manager to think about growth as well as recession when reading this chapter.

The key steps in managing through the business cycle are the following:

1. Assess the company's vulnerability to recession.
2. Sketch out a contingency plan for dealing with recession.
3. Build flexibility into the day-to-day operations.
4. Develop an early warning system for identifying coming downturns.

This chapter deals with the first three items on the list. The assessment will show the business leader how significant the pain of a downturn could be. The contingency plan begins the management team's thinking about a downturn. Building flexibility into the system is part of preparing for the inevitable recession or slowdown.

In Chapter 7, you'll learn about specific steps that can be incorporated into the contingency plan, so you won't be able to complete such a plan immediately after reading this chapter. (Just be patient!) However, the idea of the contingency plan is a key step that must be taken early on, so it is described in general terms here. The fourth action step, development of an early warning system, is so important that a full chapter (Chapter 6) is devoted to it.

THE VULNERABILITY ASSESSMENT

"How vulnerable is our company to recession or a slowdown in sales?" This question must be asked by anyone in a position of authority. The chief executive officer must ask the question, but all other executives must also incorporate the answer into their planning. The chief financial officer will be a key player in getting the company through a slow-down. The operations head is likely to bear the brunt of cost cutting. The staff functions, such as human resources, will implement many of the steps that need to be taken, and they may also have to reduce staff. Marketing and sales will be working in a very different environment when a recession comes. Research and development teams would like to be insulated, but certain products are more desirable in a recession than in a boom, and staff cuts in research and development are common during downturns.

Looking at the business's own history of dealing with downturns is a nice idea, but that's usually not practical. First, many businesses are too young to have a history covering more than a couple of recessions. A business begun in 1985 has been through only two recessions as of 2006.

Even a business with a long history needs to be cautious about using its own past. Note that use of the company's historical experience could be quantitative, as when an analyst examines actual sales figures from past eras, or it could be qualitative, as when a seasoned executive remarks, "We usually don't have much of a problem in recessions." The first practical problem is that many businesses with long histories have changed sufficiently that their old sales patterns don't reflect current sensitivities. One of my clients in the plywood industry used to sell to wholesalers but now sells considerable volume directly to big box retailers such as Home Depot. Eliminating the middleman may have altered the timing between overall economic changes and company sales. Other businesses have significantly changed their product mix. IBM used to earn most of its revenue selling hardware; now it makes a majority of its revenue providing services. The cyclical pattern of that company has certainly changed as a result of the new business model.

Finally, many businesses have not saved their historical records. Annual data on sales are not nearly as useful as monthly data, but many people in accounting don't see a need to save monthly data once the annual totals have been calculated. Because data warehouse strategies are fairly new, many businesses simply can't say how their sales fluctuated when they were entering the 1973–1975 recession—or even the 1990–1991 recession.

The best gauge of vulnerability, then, is often national data on the company's industry. To start a search for industry data, identify your business's category in the North American Industry Classification System (NAICS), which is now the standard classification. (See *www.businomics.com* for a link to more information about NAICS.) This system replaces the Standard Industrial Classification (SIC). The old SIC system may have to be used for historic data in some cases.

In addition, identify which component of gross domestic product includes your company's sales. If the end users of the product are consumers, the likely sources of information are the Census Bureau's retail sales and the National Income and Product Accounts data. The Resources section of *www. businomics.com* shows the major sources of government data on economics.

Once the pieces of data are in hand, they should be analyzed to answer the following questions:

- How much do sales in our industry decline in recession? What's the worst that has happened in the past?
- Does our industry go into recession before, at the same time, or after the national economy goes into

recession? If earlier or later, how many months of difference is there?

■ Does our industry recover from recession before, at the same time, or after the national economy? Again, what's the difference in months?

■ How long does it usually take our industry to recover from a recession?

As an example of how to answer these questions, I did a sample case study on the recreational boat industry and found the following:

■ In recessions, sales of recreational boats decline 31 percent, on average, from the best month before the recession hits, to the worst month within the recession. In the worst experience on record, sales dropped 48 percent.

■ Boat sales hit their peak about four months before the economy hits its peak. News about the national economy going into recession comes too late to help the boat industry. Boat industry recessions last, on average, fifteen months (measured on a peak-to-trough basis).

■ The industry's trough comes at about the same time as the end of the national recession, so news of a national rebound will mean that the boat industry is also looking up.

■ Although boat sales begin to recover just as the national economy recovers, it takes twenty-two months from the worst month of the recession until sales regain their prior peak. Thus, the average recreational boat industry recession has fifteen down months, followed by twenty-two recovery months, at which time sales are back at their previous peak level.

The full case study can be found at *www.businomics.com.*
For businesses engaged in contingency planning for strong growth, the recession vulnerability analysis is still useful. Companies that have the sharpest downturns tend to also have the most pronounced upturns. If the survey of industry performance in past recessions shows little vulnerability, then don't expect to find a surprisingly strong response to an economic resurgence, either.

BUSINOMICS CHECKLIST FOR VULNERABILITY TO RECESSION

▶ Here are some things to explore when assessing your company's ability to withstand a recession:

- Identify major products and services.
- Compile the company data. Find historical data on company's sales monthly (preferred) or quarterly, since at least 1979. If there have been major changes in type of product or service sold, abandon this approach.
- Find government data on the industry.
- Find relevant industry data from trade associations.
- Determine industry vulnerability. Using a table of business cycle dates, examine the neighborhood of each economic peak.
- Determine if your peak came earlier or later, and by how much.
- Find your trough, and determine if your trough came earlier or later.
- Calculate the percentage drop in sales (or production or employment) for your sector.
- Calculate time from trough until the sector regained its previous peak.

THE CONTINGENCY PLAN

The senior management team must sketch out a plan for recession long before any forecaster forecasts a recession. The plan's greatest value comes from thinking ahead of time about how to deal with recession. Considering this possibility can lead a manager to build flexibility into the business long before it's needed.

A thick binder filled with detailed plans is impractical. A good contingency plan for a single-line business can be sketched out in one or two pages. More complex businesses will need complex plans, of course, but the line managers should each be responsible for a one- or two-page plan.

The plan should be developed after reading Chapter 6, which details various steps to be considered in recessions. From the menu of possibilities presented in the chapter, business leaders can select the steps that best fit their circumstances. However, the plan should be sketched out long in advance of taking any action steps. Preparation of the contingency plan identifies issues where flexibility will be needed and areas in which bold moves will be necessary, as well as opportunities for growth that may occur. Having these in mind early will get the company through hard times better than on-the-fly management.

BUILDING FLEXIBILITY INTO THE BUSINESS

Preserving the company's options for dealing with difficult times is a major responsibility of senior management in good times. Various business arrangements limit flexibility. Some companies enter into "take-or-pay" contracts with their vendors. The vendor agrees to supply a certain amount of a raw material, and in exchange, the company agrees to either buy all of a specified amount or to make a payment to the vendor, often equal to the cost of actually purchasing the materials. Take-or-pay contracts certainly have some advantages in assuring a supply of a critical material and specifying the cost in advance. They are not uniformly bad. But they limit the buyer's flexibility. If the company's sales turn down and it does not need the raw material, then expenses cannot be cut proportionately with the production decline. If the product price falls on the spot market, then the company with a take-or-pay contract has higher prices than its competitors without such contracts. Take-or-pay contracts must be assessed with an eye not only to assuring a supply of materials at a reasonable cost, but also with regard to the difficulties they could cause in a business downturn.

Unionized companies may enter into labor agreements committing them to a certain staffing level or to generous add-on unemployment benefits. There are usually some advantages to the company from such contracts. If these provisions were not agreed to, something even more expensive might have been required to gain union acceptance of the contract. However, the loss of flexibility must be explicitly considered within the company's decision-making process.

General Motors has committed the greatest foolishness imaginable in limiting its flexibility through its "Jobs

Bank" program. Ford and Chrysler have similar programs, but GM's is the largest by far. Detroit automakers spend at least $1.4 billion a year paying workers not to work. The idea had some logic back in the old days. GM wanted more flexibility in its labor rules to increase productivity. The unions were afraid that their members would lose their jobs. A compromise was reached whereby the company would pay full wages and benefits to workers who were not needed. The idea was that the excess labor would be temporary, until sales rebounded sufficiently that GM would need all of its workers, even at a higher level of productivity. However, this program depended critically on a forecast of future sales, which includes both a forecast of the market and a forecast of GM market share. When the forecasts proved to be overly optimistic, the company lacked the flexibility to cut expenses.

The inflexible labor contract led GM to another faulty decision: continue producing cars even when demand is weak. Because it could not cut its labor costs, the marginal cost of making a new car was simply materials expense. Selling cars at large discounts, through rebates, zero-interest loans, or employee pricing, yields a price that fails to cover all costs but that does cover materials costs. In the short run, it's logical to sell cars at any price above materials costs, given the labor contract. But that practice led to perennial weak pricing of cars. During the weak markets, so many cars were sold that there was little backlog of demand when the economy improved. Much of the backlog of demand was filled by late-model used cars coming off the car-rental lots. They had been pushed to the rental companies at low prices during the weak markets, and then they ruined the strengthening markets. In short, GM failed to recognize the value of flexibility in a world with imperfect forecasts. The corporation suffered for this error.

Other commitments to fixed expense also limit flexibility. A long-term lease on real estate limits the company's ability to rent less space in a downturn. Usually the terms are so much better from a long-term lease that it is a worthwhile contract, but again, this decision needs to be made with an understanding that it has an associated cost in loss of options for the company in a recession.

Because of the close connection between these spending decisions and the business's financial flexibility, the purchasing department and the financial planning department must work together closely to obtain the best combination of low expenses plus future flexibility.

> **"Relationships with vendors and customers need to be managed in the good times with an eye to survival in the bad times."**

Relationships with vendors and customers need to be managed in the good times with an eye to survival in the bad times. In good times, vendors should be paid promptly, especially small and medium-sized vendors. That practice will pay off in goodwill when times turn hard. In other ways, the business should work to be the vendor's preferred customer. When the downturn comes, the vendor may have to make some hard choices about where to extend credit. The company may need product-development assistance from the vendor, rush deliveries, and so on. Building up goodwill in good times often allows a withdrawal from the "goodwill piggy bank" in bad times. Vendors should also be evaluated in terms of which would be best to keep in a downturn. If three vendors are providing similar goods and services, it may be better to cancel one in the downturn, rather than sharing the reduction in orders among all three.

Relationships with customers should also be managed in good times with an eye on hard times. Who is worth extending extra credit to? Who will be worth giving an extra discount to? Which customers are helping you prepare for the downturn by providing good information about their own sales?

Any consideration of who the good customers are has to be based on profitability, not volume. All too often businesses identify their best customers as their largest customers. Yet these large customers often negotiate substantial volume discounts, special credit terms, customized products, nonstandard delivery, and other unprofitable concessions. Taking into account all of the terms, the largest customers may not be the most profitable—or may not be profitable at all. Although it's outside of the scope of this book, any company that hopes to really understand its business needs to have a customer profitability analysis system. A database should keep information on the revenues from each customer, as well as an estimate of the cost of serving that customer. Negotiations with customers should take into consideration how profitable each customer is.

Hiring needs to be tight well before any recession begins. In a downturn, we often see newspaper headlines about massive layoffs. It's easy to see reduced need for production workers. Less production is going on. What about other personnel, such as finance, marketing, and product-development staff? The value of these people should depend on the long-run size of the business, not the short-term level of production. But business slowdowns are when the housecleaning occurs.

The massive staff reduction really signals that management failed to do its job in the good times. If, in fact, the business is better off without these staff members, then they should have been pruned back gradually in the good times. In this context, senior managers can make clearer judgments about which functions are overstaffed and which functions are adequately staffed or even understaffed. It is far kinder to an employee to terminate the job when the economy is strong than when it is weak. Managers who allow staffing levels to become bloated, and who then fire large number of administrative staff, have failed to do their jobs and put their organization at greater risk during economic downturns.

Capital spending plans should be developed with an eye to flexibility. Recessions are hard to forecast, so anything that lengthens the time period of a capital project also increases the risk that a recession will develop while the project is under construction.

The electric utility industry was regularly whipsawed by unexpected declines in demand growth in the 1980s and 1990s. The industry's problems were twofold. First, it took providers years to see the effects of price hikes on consumer demand. People have a hard time cutting back on electricity usage in the short run but a much easier time adjusting in the long run. After several years at higher electricity prices, people add insulation and buy more energy-efficient appliances. As a result, the electric companies were not planning on sales weakening, which eventually happened. The second part of the utilities' problem was their preference for large billion-dollar power plants. Those large plants typically had operating costs much lower than a small plant—economies of scale, in economic jargon.

However, technical efficiency doesn't count for much if the customers don't need half of the installed capacity. After sales growth slowed, the industry was caught with excess capital equipment. They learned that it's better to have slightly more expensive facilities that are heavily utilized than highly efficient plants that sit idle. Over time, the electric industry has switched to smaller, more modular generators. These are primarily gas turbines, with some natural-gas diesels providing peaking capacity. Their price tags are smaller, and, more importantly, their construction cycles are much shorter. That means that installation of the new facility begins much closer to the time of actual need. With gas turbines, two years of lead time is generally enough, compared to ten years with the largest power plants. There is far less room for forecasting error in a two-year demand analysis than a ten-year projection. As a result, the smaller plants are much more likely to be fully utilized. They are not quite as efficient as the large plants, but their flexibility more than outweighs the cost disadvantage.

Chart 5.1 shows the old electric-utility model emphasizing big generating plants. New plants are built as demand approaches capacity. When demand slows, though, the company has excess capacity for a long time. Chart 5.2 shows the same demand pattern. This company, however, has little excess capacity when demand slows.

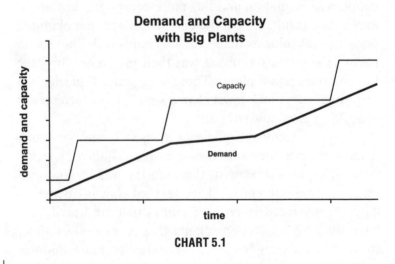

**Demand and Capacity
with Big Plants**

CHART 5.1

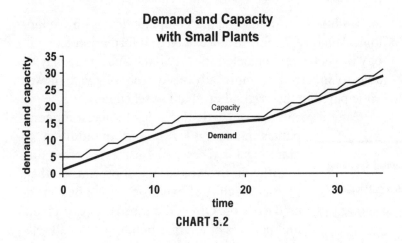

Demand and Capacity with Small Plants

CHART 5.2

The lesson for non-electric-utility businesses is also to think in smaller and more modular increments. Lay out a desired capital project and ask if it can be built in stages. Ideally, each stage should be valuable in its own right, with the next stage optional. For example, conversion to a new data system can sometimes be done in modules. Eventually, a customer-relationship management component allows orders to be passed to a production planning system, to an inventory management system, a billing system, a general ledger, and an accounts payable system. However, there may be value in upgrading individual components even before the entire system is connected together.

With modular projects, if a downturn develops before the entire series of projects is completed, the firm can halt capital spending, wait for better times, then complete the remaining modules later. Not all capital projects will fit this pattern, and sometimes the extra costs of modularity are too high. However, management should explicitly weigh the costs and benefits of flexibility before making a major capital decision.

Modularity can also help a company deal with technological change. If, for instance, a large information-technology project is implemented in stages, the final stage may be able to incorporate more advanced technology than was anticipated in the original production schedule.

Capital spending is a particular area of interest for companies planning for booms in addition to planning for recession. Businesses often find it difficult to expand the footprint of their physical facility if expansion was not considered early on. Often, the expense of extra land, and perhaps of a larger building, is small relative to the cost of adding on at a later time. In this situation, planning for the boom tends to conflict with planning for the recession. Minimizing expense is good for the recession, but maximizing the ability to expand is good for the boom. There is no answer that is always right, but business leaders must consider these issues when making their decision. It usually turns out to be a judgment call, but judgment always looks better when all factors have been considered.

> **"Capital spending is a particular area of interest for companies planning for booms in addition to planning for recession."**

Finally, the flexibility effort should evaluate current funding sources for adequacy in a recession. Funds, obviously, come from issuing equity or debt, as well as from current cash flow. Possible sources of cash need to be considered with an eye to how well they will meet the company's needs in a recession. If current funding sources may not be adequate, other options should be considered now, when times are good.

Most bank loans are for a limited term, such as a year. A company caught in a downturn may have trouble renewing the loan at the end of its term. Even long-term loans often have covenants requiring the company to maintain certain financial conditions. For example, a loan agreement may include a covenant that income available to service debt be at least 1.5 times debt service requirements. Another typical covenant is a minimum level of net worth. These covenants may be hard to meet in a recession.

The obvious options for increasing financial flexibility are issuing equity, long-term debt, or paying a fee for a stand-by credit line. It may feel like an unnecessary expense to pay a loan commitment fee on a line of credit that will never be used. It will certainly feel uncomfortable paying a higher interest rate on a long-term bond when short-term bank debt is currently available at a lower interest rate. Paying fees for future flexibility, though, is as prudent as buying insurance. The Penn Central Railroad offers a dramatic case in point.

Back in 1970, the Penn Central was financing a large portion of its operations with commercial paper. (Commercial paper is a short-term loan, usually for three to six months, in which a large corporation borrows from large institutions.) The recession of 1970 lowered freight traffic and thus Penn Central's revenue and internal cash flow as well. Penn Central's creditors got nervous about the railroad's ability to repay its debt, and they refused to roll over $82 million of commercial paper. The railroad went bankrupt. Had the Penn Central financed its operations with bonds, the creditors would not have been able to pull the plug on their financing, and Penn Central might well have survived until the economy rebounded in late 1971.

The potential difficulty of refinancing maturing debt leads to another lesson for contingency planning: When financing with bonds, make sure that the maturities are staggered. Having two or three bonds all come due in the same year is a formula for disaster if that year happens to be in a recession. Having at least two years between maturities is necessary for all but the largest corporations (which may not be able to avoid having bonds mature almost every year).

Throughout the good times, management needs to keep in mind the potential for a serious decline in sales. It's common when business is going well for people to assume that their own talents are generating success and that there is no reason to expect a change. But humility should be the watchword at companies that set themselves up to survive in difficult times. The task of management in good times is not only to exploit the current environment, but also to prepare for a new environment. Part of the preparation must deal with possible recession. Business leaders exhibit leadership when they consider *ahead of time* the decisions they may be called to make when things are difficult.

KEY POINT

Many ordinary business decisions limit or increase flexibility in the future. All such decisions need to be made with a conscious understanding of how much flexibility is being gained or lost.

SUMMING UP

Planning for a recession begins with an understanding of how vulnerable an enterprise is to a downturn. After the vulnerability assessment, some companies will sketch out only cursory contingency plans and will add only limited flexibility to their operations. Other businesses, however, will realize the serious risk that they face and undertake more thorough planning and incorporate flexibility-enhancing decisions throughout their operation. The most valuable part of the contingency-planning process is thinking through your options. The lessons from contingency planning flow through to the next step, building flexibility into the business. A company that learns in its contingency planning that it has limited options for cutting expenses may spend a year adding flexibility wherever it can, ending up with a business fairly able to cut expenses in a downturn. In fact, a good deal of flexibility can usually be obtained fairly easily, once senior executives start looking for options to do so.

CHAPTER 6

BUSINOMICS

The Early Warning System: Radar for Business

WILLIAM B. CONERLY, PH.D.—In 1940, the Battle of Britain began as 2,400 Luftwaffe aircraft attacked England. The Royal Air Force had only 900 planes, yet they successfully defended their country from the Germans. The key to their success, as every schoolchild knows, was radar. The British had early warnings of German attacks, allowing them to use their assets to great advantage. This chapter is about "radar for business"—your early warning system.

Sales will invariably speed up or slow down. Sometimes the changes are temporary blips, but sometimes the first changes presage major swings in direction. A company can respond quickly or slowly, and quickly is almost always better. On the upturn, slow-acting companies risk not being able to meet their customers' needs. Market share will fall and, even worse, the business may acquire a reputation for being an unreliable vendor. When sales turn down, the company is at risk of having excess inventories and financial commitments that it cannot fulfill. In either case, fast response to a new environment is the key to thriving and, sometimes, even surviving.

An early warning system gives management the earliest possible signals of a change in the sales environment. The system should also be set up to signal changes in costs. A monitoring system should have four parts:

- Macroeconomic warning signals
- End-user information
- Customer sales forecasts
- Critical costs

Whether the system is simple or complex, it must be executed regularly and consistently. Regularity is vital because good intentions fall by the wayside when people get busy. A New Year's Day commitment to watch the economy is about as useful as any other New Year's resolution. In order to guarantee that the task gets done, the discipline of a monthly or quarterly schedule is vital.

Consistency is the greatest value to look for in early warning reports. It ensures that the person preparing the report has not selectively chosen the most optimistic, or the most pessimistic, indicators. This may not be done intentionally, but it's natural for human beings to seize upon information that confirms their prior opinions and to overlook evidence to the contrary. A casually prepared report may contain the quarterly GDP data one month, then consumer confidence the following month, followed by retail sales the third month. Although these three data series are correlated, one of them is always showing somewhat better information than the others. Picking and choosing indicators from month to month places the company at risk of a biased view.

Consistency of the report forces executives to look at the bad news as well as the good.

The purpose of the early warning system is to help management face the reality of the external environment. Too many corporations have management teams that simply reinforce the beliefs of the chief executive officer. A standard economic report forces the entire management team to look at information that may be contradictory to the boss's preconception, and the business can only benefit from this.

KEY POINT
The early warning report should be prepared consistently and regularly.

MACROECONOMIC WARNING SIGNALS

The macroeconomic component of the early warning system watches the overall economy and the major sector most relevant to the company. The system picks up a broad-based slowdown in economic activity. At the level of specific economic sectors, it should identify when buyers are speeding up their spending or slowing it down. However, this level of detail will not identify buyers switching from, say, cars to clothing.

The macroeconomic indicators that a firm selects to monitor can be as simple as the manager keeping an eye on the news, or they can be sufficiently sophisticated that a professional economist is hired. I recommend that the early warning system be formalized, for the sake of regularity and consistency described above. However, it can be simple. Just a few charts or lines of data can cover the major data series that show changes in the economy.

Monitoring economists' forecasts can be helpful. Though the profession does not have a perfect track record at forecasting recessions, it does have a good track record at anticipating slowdowns. Recall that a recession is an officially defined contraction, requiring both depth of decline and breadth of decline across most of the economy. A slowdown is simply a slowing of the growth rate. Even though forecasting a recession is hard, forecasting a slowdown is relatively easy. In the beginning of 2001, the economy was not in recession. The fourth quarter 2000 data had not been released, but would, in time, show that the economy had grown by 2.2 percent in twelve months. Forecasters were nervous, however. The consensus forecast published by the Federal Reserve Bank of Philadelphia in February 2001 predicted a mere 0.8 percent growth in the first quarter. Also of significance, the forecasters had revised their numbers down from 3.3 percent growth in the prior survey three months earlier. That should have been a tip-off that the economy needed watching. The forecasters anticipated a rebound later in 2001, which proved to be far from the actual case. However, executives who saw the lowered forecast in early 2001 and thereafter watched the economy closely were in a far superior position to those managers who chugged forward as if nothing were amiss.

For firms that are very sensitive to the economy, a slowing of growth may be as bad as a recession. For firms that are relatively immune to recession, the forecast of a slowdown in growth rates should be taken as an indication that continued observation is needed.

A "consensus forecast" provides the best look at the future. Studies of forecast accuracy have found that the average of a group of forecasts is generally more reliable than any one particular forecaster. The best known is Blue Chip

Economic Indicators, which collects a number of forecasts and publishes the average, along with various other statistics about the forecasts.

Be wary of an individual forecast highlighted in a newspaper or magazine article. Professional forecasters are usually clumped together near the consensus, with a few forecasters at the extremes of optimism and pessimism. A reporter who wants to file a story with a particular slant can usually find someone to support that view, even if the broad community of professional forecasters disagrees. Thus, the newspaper or magazine article may only be telling you what the journalist went looking for. Also, bear in mind that news stories are often more interesting if they feature an offbeat forecast

BUSINOMICS CONSENSUS ECONOMIC FORECASTS

- *Blue Chip Economic Indicators* is the best-known consensus, published monthly by Aspen Publishers, Inc.
- *BusinessWeek* magazine annually compiles a large number of forecasts twice a year, typically in their first issue of the year and in July.
- Consensus Economics, Inc., publishes monthly consensus forecasts for the United States and other countries.
- *Survey of Professional Forecasters*, is published quarterly by the Federal Reserve Bank of Philadelphia and is free.
- The *Wall Street Journal* compiles a large number of forecasts twice a year, typically in the first issue of the year and the first issue of July. Regular updates are available to subscribers on the *Journal*'s Web page.

Links to these reports appear in the Resources section of *www.businomics.com*.

or an unusual view. Thus, the extreme ends of the distribution get far more attention than they deserve. It's best to use a bit of a "buyer beware" approach when it comes to seeking out information.

The moral is that news reports are not a reliable way to stay in touch with *conclusions* about the economic outlook, though they are reliable about the basic facts of the economic news. This is all the more reason to stay in touch with the consensus forecast.

In addition to watching forecasts, it is vitally important to watch the actual data as they are released by the source agencies, mostly government departments. Rather than just looking at the newspaper headline on GDP growth in the most recent quarter, it's better to log in that number on an economic summary sheet. This provides a discipline to keep track of the important information.

The information in this early warning system can be presented in a table, but most people are more comfortable with visual learning. Once the charts are set up with data laid out in a spreadsheet, updating them with additional data is easy. Including charts makes for a lengthier report, but the report will be easier to skim. I like to annotate the charts by hand. Those who have easy access to a color printer may want to set up danger zones in red and caution zones in yellow, with "sweet spots" for the indicators in green.

The four charts reproduced on page 134 are part of an early warning system for a business in the pleasure boat industry. (You can see the entire sample early warning system at *www.businomics.com*.)

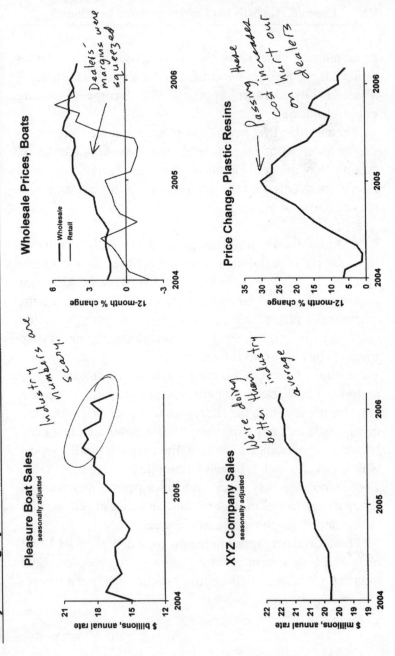

Early Warning System: Pleasure Boat Industry

Month, Year

Pleasure Boat Sales
seasonally adjusted

$ billions, annual rate

Industry numbers are scary!

Wholesale Prices, Boats

12-month % change

Wholesale
Retail

Dealers' margins were squeezed

XYZ Company Sales
seasonally adjusted

$ millions, annual rate

We're doing better than industry average

Price Change, Plastic Resins

12-month % change

Passing these cost increases hurt our dealers

END-USER INFORMATION

The next part of the monitoring system focuses on the end user. Companies close to the ultimate customer, such as retailers, need to watch proximate influences on consumer spending. Producers of intermediate goods need to watch consumption of the goods that use their product. For instance, the bottle company needs to watch sales of beer and soft drinks. A fabric manufacturer needs to watch apparel sales.

Capital goods manufacturers need to watch the end users of the products that their machinery produces. Thus, the company making semiconductor-chip manufacturing equipment should monitor closely the demand for chips, as swings in that demand will affect the need for new manufacturing equipment.

The general rule, then, is to watch the end user of your product, no matter how far removed from that end user you are.

Those firms that want a detailed forecast of their end users will probably have to subscribe to a service. They are not cheap, but they may be worth the money. The best-known firms in the business are Global Insight, Macroeconomic Advisers, and *Economy.com*. However, some of the consensus forecasts include projections for major sectors, such as consumer spending. They do not show significant detail, such as consumer spending on clothing and apparel. For that, one needs to pay a forecasting service.

Some industry trade associations employ an economist, or even a team of economists, to produce a forecast for the industry. That's a good starting place, and the forecast is usually proved free to association members. Companies have to understand, however, the constraints under which the association economist works. Oftentimes, associations want a forecast that will paint the industry in the best possible light. In some cases, a forecast of industry conditions is also a forecast of the desirability of customers buying the product. For instance, a forecast of decline in real estate values or stock market prices will discourage investors, so don't expect a trade association whose members sell real estate or investments to issue too gloomy a report. The association is in a conflicted position, and its forecast must be taken with a grain of salt.

The budget-conscious company will emphasize actual data and skip the industry forecast. The appendix to this book shows various government data sources. Trade associations often provide information about activity within their industries. For the pleasure-boat example, we focused on consumer spending. The price information includes a measure of boat prices, but production costs are presented separately. The consumer price information helps the company management understand what is driving changes in sales.

With industry data, companies can estimate their market share, which is critical to interpreting their own performance. Businesses that are unable to find good industry data may have to rely on competitive information. If major competitors are publicly traded companies, watching their financial reports may be valuable. For companies that are not publicly traded, sometimes information can be gleaned from vendors or from regulatory filings.

KEY POINTS

The end user may not be your customer.	Companies need to monitor the buying ability and levels of their end users.

CUSTOMERS

The third part of the monitoring system keeps in touch with the firm's own customers. A system needs to be in place to report to management both the sales that are currently occurring and expectations of future sales.

The current sales report should be broken down by significant customer and product groups. Commonly, a significant change in total sales can be traced to one particular product or region. Drilling down to the source of a sales growth or decline can help determine whether a new trend is in place or whether the change is just a temporary aberration. A balance is needed, however, between detail and aggregation. The most useful reports have a high-level summary by major products and, perhaps, regions. Backing up the aggregation is the ability to look at the details. The best practice is usually to provide the senior management team with the summary and with a staff analysis about the details behind the summary. By "staff analysis," we mean a paragraph at most about any significant results from the drill down. Most months, the drill down probably won't be necessary.

A good staff analysis only looks at figures that are important, usually because of significant changes, and always because the line item is important to the firm. The analysis must answer: *Do we have a change in the environment, or do we have a blip?* Examples of blips would be a large, recurring order booked later than normal, so that sales look soft one month but rebound sharply the next month. Or a large, nonrecurring order might show up as a sales gain. Whatever the case, the analysis explains whether the figure is important or not.

The staff analysis to be avoided looks like the "discussion" section of a financial statement, in which words are used to describe a table of numbers. Don't write a paragraph telling the reader that sales of widgets were up—that is evident in the table. Tell the reader whether the increase is a one-time blip or the beginning of an upward trend.

Most businesses will, from time to time, add new products, new territories, or new marketing channels. A hot new product poses a risk, however. Rising sales for the new gadget may mask a general downturn in the business. Let's say that do-it-yourself homeowners are cutting back on their spending, but your company has just introduced the coolest cordless drill ever designed. Total sales may be propelled up even in a declining market. That's great, but it places the company at risk of not realizing that its basic market is weakening. That is why a good sales tracking system has to show new products and new markets as separate items.

Many companies should include sales forecasts as well as actual sales data in the early warning system. A variety of ways are used to develop forecasts, and in this chapter we'll just scratch the surface. However, even companies with solid sales tracking and forecasting systems will want to pay attention to the elements necessary for a good early warning system. A forecasting system that is good for one purpose may need adjusting to suit the needs of an early warning system.

The companies that will benefit most from sales forecasts are those selling to other companies or to consumers on large-ticket projects that involve a long sales process, such as home remodeling.

For business-to-business commerce, there are several approaches to forecasting. One common approach is a pipeline report. Every sales representative enters into a database every prospect, the dollar amount of the sale anticipated, the probability of getting the sale, and the likely final decision date. Simple arithmetic, multiplying dollar amounts by probabilities, produces a dollar sales forecast. This well-respected approach needs some understanding before it can be incorporated into an early warning system.

Sales representatives estimate their own probability of success on each project and how large each project will be. Some natural optimism should be expected here. Most successful salespeople are optimistic. That's the nature of great salespeople, but it works against accuracy in the forecast. I have remarked to fellow consultants that proposals that seem to me to be 90 percent likely to be accepted actually fail about 30 percent of the time. So those projects really had only a 70 percent chance of success, but they sure seemed to me at the time to be 90 percent likely. Estimates of dollar volume may also be optimistic. This inherent inaccuracy leads some companies to toss out the system. As an input to, say, a production planning model, the pipeline forecast could very well lead to hideous overproduction.

"Sales representatives estimate their own probability of success on each project and how large each project will be."

In the early warning system, however, a persistent bias is not necessarily a problem. The early warning report should track changes in the pipeline forecast from one month to another. If two monthly forecasts have the same proportionate bias, then comparison of the reports will show the underlying trend.

Businesses with ongoing rather than project-by-project sales need input from their customers to form a sales forecast. Examples of such companies include a company that provides sheet metal to an appliance manufacturer, or a wholesaler that provides fresh fish to restaurants. Building a good relationship with the customers is critical if the information they provide is to be unbiased. If the customer's plans are treated as a firm commitment, the customer may lowball to avoid unnecessary obligation. If the customer's plans are taken as a hold on product, then the customer may exaggerate expectations to ensure adequate supply. Neither of these alternatives provides good information. Instead, forecasts should be treated simply as information, and the customer should be encouraged to present honest expectations. This may require some trust building. It may come from experience, but the trust comes faster if the supplier knows from the outset that honest information is one goal of the relationship. If the customer is hesitant to say anything, then the salesperson assigned to the account should try to translate the customer's casual comments into a sales forecast.

Firms that may skip sales forecasts are those selling directly to the mass consumer market. Although a large retail grocer needs a sales forecast for specific products, that sales forecast probably will not include any information not already in the early warning system. Adding up the individual product sales forecasts is thus redundant.

For purposes of the monitoring system, it's imperative for management to hear about sales slowdowns immediately. The sales manager who tells his troops to work harder and conceals the weak sales from upper management is a threat to the survival of the company. Management needs to know when to start hunkering down, and members of the sales staff have the ears closest to the customer.

At times of crisis, the chief executive officer may be in the best position to play this role—but usually only after the failure of routine systems. EMC Corporation, which makes computer storage devices, started losing sales in early 2001. The sales managers diagnosed the problem as a temporary blip in an upward-trending sales path. The new CEO, Joe Tucci, started calling on the chief executive officers and chief financial officers of EMC's largest clients. This put his information source one or two levels above the technology department managers with whom the salespeople were speaking. Tucci learned startling news: that EMC was not in the midst of a blip, but in a major structural change regarding how corporations spent their technology dollars. Tucci restructured the company to reflect his customers' new directions and brought the firm back from the brink of disaster. Such a CEO-as-savior story may be heartwarming, but it is by no means a reliable business strategy. A much better idea is gathering critical information on a routine basis, so that the company is saved through routine procedures, not heroic efforts.

Many managers tend to think, "I keep track of this stuff. I'm doing this. I just don't write it down in a formal process." There are substantial benefits to some formal process here. First, it requires the management team to determine exactly what concepts they need to track. The casual approach leads to a mish-mash of random variables. The formal process also provides a discipline to ensure that the early warning system is monitored regularly. Make it a part of one monthly managers' meeting so that it is never forgotten.

KEY POINTS

Current sales reports should include a "drill-down" of major surprises.	Product and regional breakdowns must be used when new products or territories are added.	Pipeline forecasts are useful for companies making large one-time-only sales.	Sales forecasts should be developed in consultation with customers for ongoing sales.

COSTS

Some, but not all, companies should include costs elements in their early warning system. The companies that need to pay the closest attention to costs are usually manufacturers, contractors, or utilities with significant exposure to one or two raw materials with typically volatile prices. These types of companies can be caught by surprise by cost increases.

Other businesses, however, buy a diversified mix of services and commodities and are not likely to be surprised. An accounting firm may be hurt by rising wages for accountants, but the problem will arise gradually. It is a problem that must be managed, but it comes at a pace that does not require costs to be on an early warning system. A hospital purchases many types of products, from drugs to cleaning supplies to food to linens. Although cost control is important, there are few costs that can rise sharply in the short run that would seriously hamper business plans.

The general rule of thumb, then, is to include in the early warning system any cost that is a large portion of operating expenses and which has a history of sharp changes in direction, either upward or downward.

KEY POINT

You should put costs in the early warning system if your company's expenses are dominated by one or a few major items subject to large price swings.

SEASONAL ADJUSTMENT

Many businesses have pronounced seasonality in their sales. Obvious examples are food-processing activity around harvest time, jewelry sales around Christmas, and home remodeling in the spring and summer. Most other businesses have a noticeable seasonal pattern, even if they are not so obvious. Bank deposits, for instance, have a seasonal pattern associated with both spending patterns and tax payment dates. Oil-change shops see stronger business in the summer as people prepare their cars for vacation travel. Whatever the business, sales must be tested for seasonality, and any seasonality found in the data adjusted for. A rough idea of seasonality of the economy shows up in the national employment data for one year.

CHART 6.1

Analyzing unadjusted data on the chart would show that employment grew by 3.2 percent from January through June, which sounds good. However, January is usually a slow month, and June is typically a strong month. After taking into account the typical season pattern, the adjusted data show a mere 0.8 percent gain.

Businesses can take seasonal patterns into account in several different ways. The most basic is for experienced managers to just know what the pattern is by the seat of the pants. In Chapter 1, I told the story of the experienced manager who had acquired a seat-of-the-pants knowledge of the company's seasonal patterns. There are, as the story explained, drawbacks to this approach.

Calculating twelve-month percentage changes removes seasonal movements. June of one year is compared to June of the preceding year, so it's an apples-to-apples comparison. This approach is simple and intuitive. Unfortunately, a change in trend will only show up after twelve months, which is often too late.

A visual approach shows several years of data plotted over a calendar year. Chart 6.2 shows that in 2004, employment began rising above the previous year's level, with the growth trend continuing into 2005. This approach is simple, but it leads the observer to compare this year's data with last year's data. If last year's data includes an unusual month, the eyeball will compare new data to that unusual data.

BUSINOMICS JARGON MADE CLEAR: *SEASONAL ADJUSTMENT*

▶ This term describes the statistical process whereby normal seasonal fluctuations are removed from the data so that a change from one month to the next reflects everything except normal seasonal fluctuation. For example, jewelry sales rise 34 percent from November to December. However, in past years, sales have risen an average of 37 percent during the same season. In this example, the seasonally adjusted sales would show a 3 percent decline (34 percent actual minus 37 percent normal). Actual calculations are more complex.

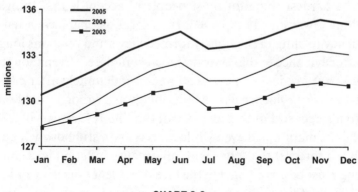

CHART 6.2

A good eyeball will examine several years of data intuitively, but this approach demands good judgment.

The preferred approach is to perform a seasonal adjustment on the data. The actual process is a bit convoluted, even using the Census Bureau's software, but it only needs to be done once a year. (New data can be adjusted using seasonal factors computed within the last twelve months.) A link to the free seasonal adjustment program appears in the Resources section of *www.businomics.com*.

Regardless of the method used, sales data must somehow be examined in light of normal seasonal patterns.

KEY POINTS

Many data series, such as a company's sales, have a normal seasonal pattern that must be considered when examining the data.	Seasonality can be taken into account through twelve-month percentage changes, through graphical methods, or by formal seasonal adjustment.

SUMMING UP

The hardest thing for most people to accept is that things don't always go as expected. In general, people have a tendency to cling to previously formed views and opinions long after evidence to the contrary has accumulated. Even though it is not prudent to pursue a forecast indefinitely after contradictory evidence arises, it is not always wrong to hold on to a forecast. For instance, a call that interest rates will fall can be maintained even while rates remain stubbornly high. But a forecast that rates will fall because inflation is declining must be abandoned in the face of evidence of rising inflation. So if the underpinnings of a view are proved wrong, the view itself must be abandoned.

The most successful managers are open to evidence of changing conditions. In order to make the shift from ignoring contrary evidence to acting on the new reality, several processes are helpful. First, religiously evaluate market conditions. It is easy to ignore contrary evidence, so a regular review forces an evaluation. Second, discuss the evidence with someone else. (Many of us find it easier to fool ourselves than to fool others.) Finally, a monthly review of economic information builds familiarity with the data. Along an improving sales path, there will always be disappointing months. These are just random blips, not cause for concern. It takes some experience to look at sales or economic data and identify what is most likely a random blip and what is possibly the beginning of serious problems. The longer the time period over which business leaders have been examining the data, the easier it is for them to separate the signal from the noise.

Alan Greenspan was perhaps the greatest chairman the Federal Reserve has ever had. One of the keys to his success was his familiarity with the data. Like few who came before him, Greenspan immersed himself in the data. More importantly, he had been immersed in the data for decades before he joined the Fed. His experience as an economic consultant helped him to interpret the data as the economy evolved.

Business managers don't have to aspire to be an Alan Greenspan, and they probably don't have the time to put into data analysis that Greenspan did. However, the discipline of regularly reviewing data will pay dividends in a better understanding of the unfolding economic environment.

The radar operators who first interpreted blips on radar screens needed some experience before they were adept at separating out signals—German bombers—from the noise of static and interference from ground installations. Practice made perfect, however, and Britain was saved through the use of radar. Many businesses are also saved by careful attention to the early signs of economic downturns.

Managing Through the Business Cycle

WILLIAM B. CONERLY, PH.D.—In Chapter 5, I set out the key steps for managing through the business cycle:

1. Assess the company's vulnerability to recession.
2. Sketch out a contingency plan for dealing with recession.
3. Build flexibility into the company's day-to-day operations.
4. Develop an early warning system for identifying coming downturns.

Chapter 5 also described how to assess a company's vulnerability to recession and how to build flexibility into the business. Chapter 6 explained how to construct an early warning system to spot upcoming problems. In this chapter, we'll go through the steps that your business should take when a recession or growth slowdown occurs, followed by a discussion of business challenges in an improving economy.

After the vulnerability assessment, a contingency plan should be sketched out. "Sketched out" does not mean a thick binder with detailed plans. However, it is wise to do a pro forma income and cash-flow statement on the assumption that sales fall to recessionary levels. Then the management team should identify options for limiting expenses.

Every company has a series of steps, such as a hiring freeze, that can be taken in a downturn. The easy steps should be implemented quickly when the early warning system signals caution. More severe steps, such as layoffs, will be implemented as the economic slowdown shows up in the company's actual sales reports. Finally, a company sometimes goes into survival mode, in which avoiding liquidation is the sole aim.

The same urgency is seldom needed when the economy is weak but showing signs of recovery. However, the same principles apply: Think ahead of time about the steps that you may have to take. Early consideration can help you to grow the business.

The following list of steps for thinking about a recession will not apply to all companies, but they can be used as a menu. Select your favorites, but think ahead about how you'll implement them.

Checklist for Managing in a Downturn

Here are some considerations for managing in an economic downturn:

- Capital spending: Reevaluate, limit
- Employment: Reevaluate, freeze, layoffs
- Inventories: Limit, sell excess

- Accounts receivable: Tighten terms, factor
- Relationship with financing sources: Inform throughout cycle
- Lines of business: Consider selling or closing money-losing segments

In the following sections, we'll discuss these steps, moving from the easiest to the most severe steps.

EASY STEPS

When the monitoring system signals a slowing of sales, it's time to start fine-tuning the contingency plans. Pull out the notes that, hopefully, were prepared some time in the past. Update them for recent changes in the business. Then get down to work.

Capital spending plans that are near implementation should be reevaluated. Remember our earlier discussion of modularity and flexibility in capital projects. Now is when flexibility is golden. This isn't to say that all capital spending should be stopped. First, the company's sensitivity to recession may be small. Second, there may be cost savings from the capital spending. Third, there may be costs to canceling plans. Finally, a company may judge that the potential rewards outweigh the risks, even with lower sales.

There is nothing wrong with such a judgment when formed in a discerning way. The danger, though, comes from emotional decisions. If management feels a strong emotional investment in the capital plan, then the firm is less likely to suspend the plan when it should. People who have been advocating the project may have a career investment that requires them to continue pushing the plan. A manager may also feel that he or she wants so badly for the plan to succeed that the plan becomes sacrosanct even in the light of weakening ability to afford it. However, unbiased calculation is critical when your organization is at the beginning of a downturn.

After looking at capital spending, staffing levels deserve scrutiny. Although it is probably too early at this stage to lay off people, hiring should be slowed when the early warning signs start popping up. It's often better to run some overtime than to replace normal turnover.

This is a good time to look at staffing in administrative functions. It's too early for massive layoffs, but some effort to evaluate the need for the administrative staff is appropriate. At the best companies, staff is kept lean throughout the good times. However, very few companies rate as "best" in this regard. If your firm has not done a thorough review of administrative staffing in the last two years, you are probably kidding yourself when you say that it's a lean operation. This is a good time for the review, which is likely to lead to one worker being dropped in this department, perhaps two in another department, maybe none in a third department. Carefully prune administrative staff at this time.

Inventories need to be monitored closely all of the time but especially closely after the company perceives weakness in the sales chain. The early warning signals may be unclear about whether the business slowdown is a full-blown recession or just a period of slower growth. In either case, however, sales growth will turn down in most industries. Recall the discussion in Chapter 3 about how inventory changes become magnified farther up the supply chain, away from the customer. Caution about inventories pays off. Also recall from Chapter 3 how small changes in final demand become magnified going up the supply chain. Be very careful about inventories.

Accounts receivable need more attention at this time. To begin with, credit terms should be tightened. There is usually a temptation to goose sales by offering easier terms, but that is the exact opposite of what is prudent. Most likely, your customers' credit-worthiness will be deteriorating, which indicates that credit standards should be higher than normal. This will be a frustrating time because competitors will probably be easing credit terms, and some sales may be lost. However, sales that do not result in payments are gifts, not sales.

By this time, if not before, the business should have considered selling receivables. In the finance industry, selling receivables is called "factoring." For some companies, factoring is a way of life. For others, it is an occasional activity. Factoring can help a company in temporary financial difficulties with a shot in the arm of cold cash. The cost, though, is that the factor will not pay the full value of the receivables, so the company selling receivables gets less than if it had collected the bills itself. If a company doesn't need to factor, that's great. But many companies will get into worse conditions and wish that they could quickly sell some or all of their receivables.

Setting up a factoring relationship typically takes some time, and often a long-term relationship is needed so that the factor can get an idea of the quality of the company's receivables. Even if receivables do not need to be sold at this stage, it may be wise to set up the relationship so that receivables can be factored if the downturn worsens.

Gaining further financial flexibility is important here. This may be your last chance to secure a larger credit line.

You may be able to delay some payments to vendors at this point without causing undue stress on them. It may also be possible to get some long-term debt before the downturn scares away too many lenders. If possible, set up your credit lines now.

In the months just following the 2001 recession, I spoke to a banker about how his clients were doing. Some were clearly in trouble, while others were getting along decently. The difference, he said, was that the companies that had reacted to the downturn decisively and early were the ones looking good afterward. Those companies that delayed layoffs and expense reductions were in trouble even after the recession was over. The banker said that he hated to see managers laying people off, but he hated seeing entire companies close down even more.

KEY POINT

When the early warning system begins to flash a warning, review and update the contingency plan, and . . .
- Limit new hires to vital positions.
- Reduce or eliminate capital spending plans.
- Monitor inventories closely.
- Set up credit lines if possible.

MODERATE STEPS

The moderately severe steps follow the easy steps, but with greater force. Capital spending is cut entirely, or almost entirely. If exceptions are made, they should have very immediate impact on costs or be vital to continuous operation of the company. Replacing vital equipment that has broken down might be acceptable, but repairing the gear would be better in most cases. There may be some bargains available, but if the easy steps listed above don't leave the company with strong financials, then the bargains have to be eschewed for now.

A hiring freeze is the minimum employment policy. There may be exceptions—every company has some people with unique skills who simply must be replaced—but they need to be rare and fully justified. Layoffs may be appropriate as well. The critical issue on the production floor is the rarity of the skills that current workers possess. If, for example, you have some technicians who would be very hard to replace, they should not be laid off casually. But if you have fairly generic assembly workers, easily found in the general labor pool or easily trained, then layoffs will help the business survive.

> **"Times of economic stress show just how well—or badly—the company was managing in the up cycle."**

Layoffs never come easily or without pain. There is a very natural tendency, then, for managers to delay layoffs as long as possible. When conditions clearly indicate that a layoff is needed, most managers tend to wait a little longer, hoping that the economy will quickly turn around, eliminating the need to cut staff.

However, times of economic stress show just how well—or badly—the company was managing in the up cycle. Here it is important to distinguish between production workers and staff personnel. Production workers are those people whose work is directly part of producing the products that are sold. As the production level declines, the need for production workers clearly declines as well. With fewer widgets being produced, fewer people are needed to produce widgets, to box the widgets, and to ship the widgets.

Staff work is different. Much of it is related to the ongoing activities of the firm rather than current production levels. Engineering and development of new products must continue even if current sales are weak. Marketing is vital, as much in down times as up. Finance functions, legal work, and much of human resources must continue. There will be some variation in staff workload due to the decline in production. Fewer sales implies fewer invoices to be cut. But the weak economy may also mean more effort to collect accounts receivable. Generally speaking, administrative, sales, and general staff cannot be cut by more than a small fraction of the production cutback.

Working capital will be treasured during moderately poor times. Accounts receivable must be collected as rapidly as possible, and credit terms must be very tight. On the payments side, accounts payable should be delayed to the extent possible. When dealing with small but vital vendors, however, the company may have to evaluate the financial condition of these companies. If the supplier goes under, the buyer may have even more trouble lining up a new supplier or meeting the credit terms of alternative suppliers. If this is going to be a problem, then the purchasing department needs to work with accounts payable to ensure the viability of critical vendors.

If the company pays dividends on either common or preferred stock, it's time to reconsider them. Businesses with a long, unbroken history of dividend payments won't stop payments casually. For most companies, however, dividend payments should be on the table for discussion.

Inventories must also be monitored with higher vigilance during moderate downturns. Inventories are certainly needed for continuing operations, but companies will often benefit from a new review, by new eyes, of how much inventory is being kept. That review should include raw materials and work in progress, as well as finished product. Don't neglect unnecessary inventory items. Are there components that were purchased for a product that has been discontinued? Even if you are selling them for scrap, that's better than keeping useless inventory in the back of the plant.

While looking for unnecessary assets, look at entire operations that are not providing positive cash flow. Do some of your stores cost you more than they bring in? Is there a division that is still eating up corporate cash? This is a good time for a cold, hard look at them. Certainly there are new stores that will soon be profitable and divisions that are poised for a sharp rebound. But there are also moribund operations that have little upside, which have been maintained through corporate inertia. They probably should have been shut down years before. Now is the time to take action. Not only will the business's total cash flow improve, the discontinued operations may also fetch something when sold.

Relationships with financial partners need to be maintained, even if the news being presented is not good. Banks or other lenders should be kept aware of the company's condition. Loan officers will need to deliver bad news to higher-level bank executives, and surprises are punished much more severely than well-anticipated bad news. Within a bank, officers have goals and financial plans that need to be hit. A surprise can sink a plan, and thus an executive, or at least sink her bonus. Advance knowledge of trouble allows the executive to start adjusting plans, to start preparing higher-level officers, and to look for alternative ways to meet plan.

The fear some financial officers have of this "full and early disclosure" is that the lender will tighten credit more severely than he otherwise might. The lender looks for covenant violations or other ways to pull credit commitments. The lender may not renew a credit line that is due to expire. The upside of full and early disclosure, however, is greater trust between the two parties. The lender will know that there are unlikely to be hidden or undisclosed problems. Accordingly, more flexibility may be granted to the borrowers.

KEY POINTS

The moderately severe steps taken in a recession are similar to the easy steps, but they are taken further.	Business managers should review employment, capital spending, and financing, and they should keep lenders fully apprised of conditions.

SURVIVAL STEPS

If the recession is severe enough, your company's survival may be in danger. Thus, long-term concerns become less relevant. Getting through the coming months is all that matters. The steps that need to be taken at this level of severity are harsh, but they may be necessary to avoid complete loss of shareholder value.

Lenders usually want expenses cut to the bone, but one expenditure earns their respect: bringing in an outside turnaround expert. Another person, taking a more detached view, can make the case for difficult but necessary action steps.

Here are the items to be considered, whether the outside consultant is brought in or not:

1. **Capital spending not only needs to stop, but asset sales need to be considered.** When the survival of the firm is in doubt,

it is not time to fret that the excess equipment will be worth more in the next upturn. The upturn may not come soon enough.

2. **Employment must be cut as much as possible.** Future-oriented positions, such as research and development, must be eliminated. Everyone who is not critical to the survival of the firm must be laid off. The attitude toward staff layoffs at this stage is quite distinct from the moderately severe steps described above. The key distinction is that the moderately severe steps occur with an eye toward the future. The survival steps are focused solely on near-term survival.

3. **Sales personnel will be kept, though perhaps not at previous staffing levels.** But marketing staff may have to be laid off. Further cuts in all other staff areas must be made to the maximum extent that will not cause immediate closure of the firm.

4. **The other steps described earlier**—keeping inventories lean, hoarding cash, and delaying payments—**are doubly important now.**

Finally, it may become necessary to think about selling the business—or what's left of it. This is seldom easy, especially when management has emotional ties to the company. However, the facts are the facts, and they must be faced. All too often, owners or managers think in terms of what the business used to be worth and refuse offers that reflect the current value. By refusing to deal at this time, owners or managers may actually be abandoning value that they could have reaped, but which won't be available to them a few months later.

The survival steps described above are not healthy for the long term. Selling the business to another investor or company may allow continuation without the harsh survival steps. Ultimately, more value may be gained by continuing the business as a going entity than by a doomed attempt at survival.

Survival of all businesses is not guaranteed, nor should it be. Recessions cause losses from which some companies will not recover. Keeping this in mind in the good times will help prevent the worst possibilities in the bad times.

KEY POINTS		
Companies whose survival is at risk should consider bringing in a turn-around specialist.	Expense reduction measures that are harmful in the long run may be neces-sary for short-run survival.	Selling the business may provide more shareholder value than continuing the operation until bankruptcy.

TAKING ADVANTAGE OF RECESSIONS

Before the 2001 recession, a young discount airline named AirTran Airways had a small, aged fleet of airplanes. Their forty-six aircraft averaged twenty-six years old. Five years later, after a harrowing recession and the September 11 ter-rorist attacks, AirTran had seventy-six airplanes with an average age of three years old. With new planes, fuel and maintenance costs were dramatically lower. The simple les-son: Recessions are bad for most businesses, but some com-panies can use a recession to their own advantage. AirTran entered the recession with lower operating expense, and they used their competitors' difficulties as a purchasing opportu-nity. Different companies will see different opportunities, but firms that have done a good job preparing for the recession will have the best opportunities to take advantage of a recession.

Surviving the recession is a necessary prerequisite to benefiting from a recession. Once survival is likely, then it's time to exploit the economic slowdown to improve your competitive position.

Long-term contracts should be reviewed with an eye to renegotiation. For instance, if the office lease has two more years to run, it may be possible to extend it for another ten years at a very favorable rate. The landlord looking at a high vacancy rate may want to lock in a good tenant to a longer term, especially if the building owner is thinking about selling the property. Having a lease with ten years to run is much more attractive to the potential buyer than a lease nearing expiration.

Other long-term contracts, such as with suppliers, may also be renegotiable. This could also be a good time to switch from spot-market purchases to long-term contracts, locking in favorable pricing. (But keep the value of financial flexibility in mind.)

Identifying Opportunities

A recession provides several opportunities for a company with cash or credit facilities. The most obvious is acquisition of weaker competitors. A study by the McKinsey consulting firm found that successful firms tended to do fewer acquisitions in good times (compared with their less-successful peers) but more acquisitions in bad times.

A business begins its opportunity scan by looking inward at its cash and ability to finance a purchase or capital spending. Next it should identify market segments in which it would like to be larger when the recovery comes. The segments could be geographic regions into which the company would like to expand. Or the segments could be related product lines that the company does not currently offer. The segments might also be products at alternative price points, such as an upscale model of the current product. It is also quite possible that your business wants to stay in its current segments but increase its market share.

The next step is to look for distressed competitors, property and equipment, and talent.

Not only can assets be purchased inexpensively, actual competitors can often be acquired on the cheap. However, all too often they are acquired too cheaply, too late. Many owners get in trouble in the recession because they have delayed retrenchment. They are likely to delay reevaluation of the value of their company. One of my clients decided that he liked the long-run potential of a particular industry. He had an attorney who was experienced in acquisitions team up with the head of his first acquisition in the industry. The two went looking for acquisitions in 2002, when the industry was still reeling from recession. Their report: Most owners who wanted to sell were still valuing their businesses at pre-recession prices.

Thus, deals will be hard to achieve until the owners are forced by their lenders to sell the company. Unfortunately, that is often after the company has been operating in survival mode, running down the value of the business as an ongoing entity. Therefore, the best acquisitions may be divisions of larger corporations rather than owner-managed firms. Nonetheless, a good acquisition of an owner-managed firm can sometimes be made.

Acquisitions should always be approached cautiously. Over the long run, far more money is lost doing acquisitions than is gained. Too many acquisitions are motivated by executive ego and pride rather than by hard economics. The desire to make a deal leads to paying too high a price in many cases.

One approach to acquisitions that sometimes makes sense is to look for specific production facilities rather than entire companies. This works best when a business wants to expand its capacity but not necessarily extend its product line.

Talented employees can often be hired easily, and cheaply, in a recession. For businesses that are particularly dependent on employee expertise—such as industries heavily dependent on fashion or technical innovation—acquiring talent may be the best strategy in a recession. However, you must have a reason to believe that the talent will stay once the job market turns around. Sometimes compensation can be structured to include "golden handcuffs," such as profit sharing or stock options that do not vest immediately, or bonuses structured to be paid out over time.

Pricing and Sales Strategies

Prices often weaken in recession, but businesses should be very hesitant to initiate price wars to build market share. Customers who are price sensitive when prices are falling will also be price sensitive when the market tightens and prices increase. In other words, they will leave you just as quickly as they left the previous vendor.

Predatory pricing is the label for price cuts designed to put a competitor out of business. In a recession, the companies that have the strongest balance sheets may well be able to do this. The first step, however, should be to consult with a good antitrust attorney. In many cases, price cutting is perfectly legal, but in other cases it could be against the law. And the victim could be awarded triple damages if a court finds that antitrust laws were broken. Be careful.

The greater problem with predatory pricing, however, comes from newcomers entering the business. After cutting prices to eliminate competition, the idea is to then push prices up above competitive levels. That will attract new entrants into the market, often preventing the original company from ever recovering the amount lost in a price war.

New capital equipment can often be purchased at bargain prices during recessions, but here you should be cautious. There may be bargains available, but this usually happens at a time when the industry does not need additional capacity. Thus, it's generally better to buy existing capacity from competitors than to purchase new equipment during a recession. However, there may be instances in which the specific items needed cannot be bought secondhand but are available at reduced cost in a downturn. This is particularly true of the consulting costs associated with new information technology initiatives. Thousands of person-hours may be needed to install a new database for, say, production planning. That is the kind of result that cannot be achieved through acquisition, so it is probably best to use the recession as a buying opportunity.

There are several sales opportunities that arise in a recession, mostly by taking advantages of competitors' weakness. The easiest to watch for is competitors exiting a business. Note the advice above to consider closing down money-losing operations. Your competitors may be doing just that. Some of these opportunities are obvious and are reported in the newspapers. For example, in the summer of 2004, Washington Mutual closed down fifty-three business banking offices, laying off 850 workers. (This did not happen during the depths of a recession, but the action illustrates the opportunity very well.) The action was well reported in the press, and competing banks immediately started calling on WaMu's business customers. The other banks also started calling the loan officers who were being let go. WaMu's problems became other banks' opportunities.

A layoff of competitors' sales and marketing employees is far more significant than a layoff of production employees. The latter indicates lower sales, but not necessarily less sales effort. Conditions are better when competitors are not working so hard to gather in the sales opportunities that are available in the marketplace.

Lower-quality customer service or lower-quality products may result from staff layoffs at competitors. The airlines are a great case in point. As they hit recession in 2001—or actually a depression for the industry—staffing levels were cut and customer service tanked. Complaints from late flights to missing luggage accelerated. The new discount carriers bucked this trend, picking up substantial market share in the process. The recession is a good time to stay in touch with prospects looking for remedies for their dissatisfaction.

Some competitors will tighten their credit terms in a recession, though this is more likely to occur late in the downturn, when uncollectible receivables are a major problem. It's always dangerous to ease credit terms just to hold market share, but a firm that has a well-established and statistically justified credit policy can often gain customers late in the downturn as more skittish companies overreact to credit losses.

Finally, sales forces tend to be less proactive in recession. The sales staff gets discouraged by continual failure to find customers. As sales personnel are laid off, the remaining people are spread more thinly and often become order-takers rather than prospectors. Customers looking to switch vendors or to expand their business may find they have few sales representatives really hustling to get their business.

This description of opportunities is not so rosy that anyone should look forward to a recession, but it does show that it's possible to mitigate a downturn's effects, and occasionally to even profit from it.

KEY POINTS		
Opportunities during recessions include locking in favorable pricing through long-term supply contracts and purchasing additional capacity from competitors.	Avoid price wars, which are easily started in recessions.	Look for competitors whose cutbacks have left their sales and service staffs undermanned and discouraged.

MANAGING IN THE RECOVERY

The recovery sounds good. Sales are rebounding, optimism is increasing, the light at the end of the tunnel is clearly visible and growing stronger by the day. But these are not easy times. Problems abound during the early stages of the recovery. Admittedly, some problems are better to have than others. Most businesses are better off tackling the problems of recovery over the problems of a recession. However, there are indeed problems that businesses face in recovery.

Let's assume that the firm's early warning system is showing signs of strength: improving financial condition of the end customers, perhaps an end to the decline in sales, not yet an actual increase in sales, but more interest on the part of potential customers and past customers. More requests for proposals or bids are coming in. In short, all the early warning signals are flashing green.

The critical issue is whether the business is ready for an increase in sales. "Yes, yes!" everyone screams, but stop and think. There's probably sufficient production capacity, but what about the financial effects of an increase in orders? Raw materials have to be purchased in manufacturing businesses. Inventories need to be accumulated in wholesale and retail trade. In many businesses, employment levels will have to be increased. The purchase of raw materials or inventory, plus the rehiring of laid-off employees, requires expenditures. These expenditures will almost always happen before the customer makes any payment. In other words, the company's cash position will deteriorate because of the increase in orders or sales.

Companies whose cash positions worsened in the recession now face further worsening in the recovery. That doesn't seem fair, but it does seem to be realistic. Here is where strong relationships with the bank will help. If the lender came to trust the business during the recession because the finance officer was forthright about bad news and kept information flowing, then loans will be easier to come by in the recovery. Bankers would rather stretch for a company enjoying higher orders than for a company having trouble collecting on past sales. It's best not to wait until the last minute, however. When the early warning signals indicate an upturn, sketch out some scenarios for sales increases based on past rebounds. Run a financial simulation to indicate cash needs. (A financial simulation may sound sophisticated, but it need be no more than a spreadsheet with a dozen line items.) Then talk to the banker about how these various scenarios would impact the firm's credit needs.

Key employees may have to be recalled. Most often in the downturn, a company does not cut staff as much as it cuts production, so that a fair amount of production can be restored before additional hiring is needed. This may not be true of specific skills needed, however. If one or two key technicians retired or otherwise left the firm during the downturn, then it may not be possible to turn production around on a dime. The time to evaluate personnel needs in the upturn is while in the middle of the downturn. This isn't to say that excess staffing needs to be maintained in the recession. However, management needs to know, at all times, its capability to increase production. If the departure of a key person has diminished the firm's ability to ramp up production, then the company needs to anticipate rehiring well before the need arises. Interviews with candidates for the position can be started well before the estimated hiring date. Simply disclose to the candidates that the timing of the need is uncertain. If the type of critical skills tend to be rare, it may be necessary to hire well before the need arises. More often, though, simple foresight and preparedness will prevent a problem when production does need to be increased.

The largest employment issue in the recovery is ensuring adequate labor supply a year or two down the road. As labor markets eventually tighten, employee turnover increases. Workers who are dissatisfied with their jobs will not quit during a recession, but they will be looking for alternatives as the economy improves. The time to improve employee attitudes toward the business is well before the workers have good opportunities elsewhere.

Action steps to lower employee turnover are varied, but it appears that better training of first-line supervisors often has the best bang for the buck. Some companies have lowered quit rates by better informing employees of their company benefits, even without expanding benefits. Other firms provide more in-house training or links to off-site training for employee advancement as an employee-turnover strategy. The old-fashioned approach is to offer higher wages, but management should consider lower-cost avenues first.

Other business issues can usually wait until the turnaround is well underway. Capital spending, research and development, and new marketing campaigns can usually be postponed until the company's finances are on a firmer footing. So during the recovery, management needs to focus on finance, and it needs to double-check that personnel are up to the challenge of increasing production.

KEY POINTS

Managing in a recovery begins with ensuring capacity to expand production.	Increasing sales usually stresses the company's cash position.	Expect employee turnover to increase unless significant steps are taken to retain workers.

MANAGING IN A BOOM

Good times are great, not only for the high profits and market expansion possible, but as preparation time for the inevitable slowdowns. Thus, one of the primary objectives of managers operating in a boom is to not get too carried away. The really great booms are accompanied by articles saying, "This time it's different. The boom is truly going to last forever. Things can grow to the sky. There won't be a recession again." Such articles have always been proven wrong. It may take some time, but a slowdown and even a recession will eventually come. The boom should be used to prepare for that slowdown.

Although a boom will lead to capital spending, which often stresses the company's balance sheet, this is really the time to get the business's finances in order. No banker will ever be as magnanimous in a recession as in a boom. The boom is a great time to get collateral and personal guarantees waived. Even if, for example, the personal guarantee seems negligible, ask the banker to waive it. Then, when things turn down, the personal guarantee can be offered back to the banker—in exchange for something else, like relaxation of a loan covenant.

Operations often become stressed in times of a strong market. Production managers are hustling to keep the factory running at full capacity—or, often, at above rated capacity. Vendor deliveries are slow, leading managers to carry higher inventories, to pay for rush shipments, or to occasionally have to shut down. Lack of preventative maintenance due to the frantic pace of activity triggers more unscheduled downtime. When critical personnel have to be replaced, tight labor markets often lead to higher-than-expected wages. The result is that costs rise in a boom.

Attitudes need to change in a boom. Whereas the recession leads managers to treasure sales, now they have to treasure *profitable* sales. It is common to find in a boom that there are still substantial discounts being offered, which are often relics of recent lean times. Now consider, on the one hand, that ramping production up from 90 percent of capacity to 100 percent entails disproportionately higher costs. On the other hand, at least 10 percent of sales are transacted at steeply discounted prices. Put these two factors together, and it's time to shed some customers. Reducing production and giving up the least profitable customers can lead to higher profits. This is most likely to be the case in a booming economy, though it can be true at other stages of the business cycle as well.

The boom is also the time to review the downturn contingency plan. Remember that the value of the plan is that it forces the manager to think about options and flexibility. Sketching out a contingency plan will help the manager identify the areas of the business where flexibility can be improved.

KEY POINTS		
Use the boom to get finances in order, including credit lines.	Compare the least profitable sales price to the cost of the last few percentage points of production.	Review the contingency plan for the next downturn.

SUMMING UP

Managing in a recession occurs well before and well after the actual recession. The most important element is thinking ahead about how to incorporate flexibility into the business. Beyond that, management in the recession consists of a series of steps to protect cash, each step somewhat more severe than the last. Hopefully, sales turn around before the company enters survival mode.

At the beginning of Chapter 5, we explained that a contingency plan for dealing with recession was necessary, but we cautioned against writing one until the conclusion of this chapter. Now it's time to write out one page of notes about the steps your business could take to survive, and thrive, during a recession.

Foreign Economic Cycles: The Extra Worries of the Overseas Manager

WILLIAM B. CONERLY, PH.D.—The company operating in foreign markets needs to be concerned about business cycles in other countries, and looking at the United States isn't enough. The world is, in fact, becoming more closely integrated. Correlations among the various economies of the world are increasing, meaning that we tend to move up and down together more than we used to. However, the correlation is far from perfect, and the Asian financial crisis of the late 1990s points up the occasional huge disparity in economic performance.

In 1998, the U.S. economy grew at about the same rate as the year before and the year after. Across newly developing Asia, however, a harsh depression struck. Something was going on that would not have been foreseen just by watching the American economy.

Real Economic Growth, 1998

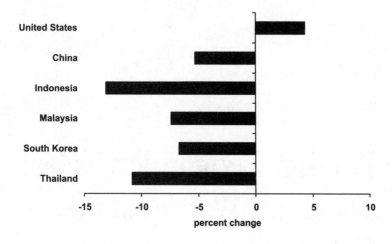

CHART 8.1

The analysis of business cycles in the preceding chapters applies about as well to other large Western countries as it does to the United States. Look for monetary policy to be a major cause of business cycles, with contributory roles from supply shocks and other factors.

In smaller and less-developed countries, though, additional factors can be at work in creating business cycles. These include commodity cycles, business cycles in major trading partners, foreign exchange crises, and political crises.

This chapter begins with a discussion of how the major business cycle factors, monetary policy, and supply shocks vary around the world. Then we go into more detail on the issues specific to smaller countries.

Managing through the business cycle in foreign countries is similar to the best practices in the United States, but there are some twists that appear in foreign operations. Often-times, the business leader will need to do more preparation to achieve the same flexibility that is easily obtained in the United States. In some countries, the same flexibility simply cannot be gained.

MONETARY POLICY AROUND THE WORLD

In the United States, the business manager needs to keep an eye on Federal Reserve policy. In other countries, the central bank will have a different name, but it will commonly play a similar role. The manner in which it plays that role, however, can be drastically different.

In the United States, the Federal Reserve has substantial independence from the president and the rest of the executive branch, as described in Chapter 3. Other countries have decidedly different systems. In many countries, policy is determined by the treasury officials. They often want to keep interest rates low in the short run, both to stimulate the economy and to lower the cost of government borrowing. Keeping interest rates low in the short run requires large increases in the money supply, which in the long run are inflationary. And in the long run, inflation means higher interest rates. But political officials are often more concerned with the short run than the long run.

Not only is formal independence of the central bank an important issue, the degree of consensus on how to conduct monetary policy is also important. In a country beset by regular debates about tight money versus easy money, expect policy to swing wildly. In a country where there is a strong political consensus for low inflation—Germany and

Switzerland come to mind here—then expect fairly stable policy.

The business implication of this structural variety is simple. When doing business in a foreign country, determine how independent the central bank is from the administration and how stable the opinion is about monetary policy. If the answer is "not very independent, not very stable," then expect greater swings in monetary policy than you see in the United States. When the administration is focused on getting people working, expect lower interest rates in the near term, with higher inflation and higher interest rates longer term. Then the administration may show more concern for inflation, with even higher interest rates near term, followed by recession.

How does an American business manager find out this information about a foreign country? As a first pass, skim articles in international publications about the country. The *Economist* is particularly good on this matter, and the *Financial Times* of London is also informative.

Reading a local newspaper may also be worthwhile. Many foreign capitals have English-language newspapers that can help. Some of those papers may be online and might have a daily e-mail news summary available.

It may be wise to hook up with an economist in the foreign country. This could be a consultant, a business-friendly professor, or an analyst with a chamber of commerce or think tank. Once the manager has a feel for how monetary policy is conducted in a given country, it's relatively easy to determine the general tenor of policy.

How much attention do you have to pay to monetary policy in other countries? I recommend thinking in terms of "idiot lights" and gauges. The idiot light in a car flashes red when there's a problem. The gauge gives more detail. When your idiot-light–equipped car is running hot, the red light goes on. When your gauge-equipped car is running hot, the needle moves up into the red zone. As a manager, you will want to set up a monitoring system that begins with an idiot light for monetary policy. That is, you want to know when and when not to pay attention to monetary policy. That doesn't require too much work. When the light flashes red—when skimming the local country news suggests that monetary policy may be changing—then it's time for more detailed consideration. That is, it's time to look at the gauge. Read the news articles more carefully, talk to local bankers and business leaders, and consult with the local economists.

KEY POINTS

In many countries, monetary policy serves short-run political interests.

Countries vary in their underlying attitudes about the role of monetary policy.

SUPPLY SHOCKS IN FOREIGN COUNTRIES

The standard supply shock from an American perspective is the oil crisis. That also applies to many, but not all, foreign countries. The severity of an oil price hike depends on a country's dependency on imported oil. The greater the dependency, the greater the harm to the country from a large increase in the price of oil.

The easy case to consider is a nation that exports oil. What is an oil price shock to consumers in the United States is a positive increase in revenue to the oil exporting country. The risks here are present though, as oil prices can fall as well as rise. I'll discuss the downside risk in the next section.

Countries totally dependent on imported oil have a greater response to supply shocks than countries with some oil, like the United States. Those countries with some oil tend to see price hikes that are every bit as large as in countries totally dependent on foreign oil. Unless the government limits the domestic oil prices, domestic oil will sell at world levels. Thus, the domestic supply does not protect the country from the oil price hike.

However, the country that is only partially dependent on imported oil has some folks benefiting from the higher oil prices. All of the oil producers in the country are better off. In the United States, for example, when the country as a whole was reeling from higher oil prices, Texas was booming. The oil patch's boom partially offset weakness in oil-consuming parts of the country.

The international business manager who sees world oil prices rising will want to take some time to look at how dependent on imported oil his key countries are. Those countries heavily dependent will feel a stronger shock; those less dependent will experience smaller effects. And those that are net exporters of oil will gain.

KEY POINT

Susceptibility to a supply depends on the country's dependence on the material in short supply (typically oil).

COMMODITY RISK IN SMALL COUNTRIES

Many smaller countries are heavily dependent on just one product. Coffee is the major crop in a number of Latin American countries. Cocoa rules in some West African nations. Oil, of course, is the primary source of income in most of the

Middle East. Countries dependent on a single product are at substantial risk from swings in the price of the product.

The good news, though, is that domestic policies may be less important. If the market for the one product is strong, it will be harder for bad monetary policy to screw things up. The overall volatility of these countries, however, will still be greater than that of countries with more diversified economies.

Price weakness can come from either of two directions: low demand or high supply. In the case of agricultural products, demand tends to be relatively stable, while supply varies widely. A good year for cocoa increases supply and drives prices down. The seeming abundance of the large harvest is more than offset by the low prices. In economic jargon, demand is relatively inelastic. That is, it takes a very large change in price to get people to change their consumption patterns. Only a very large change in price induces us to eat more chocolate than we habitually do. That large price change is very hard on the cocoa producers.

Mineral products, in contrast, are usually more stable in supply than in demand. The world's mines don't grow or shrink their underlying capacity too much from one year to the next. Yet demand for oil, metals, and other minerals can change significantly. The total level of economic activity in the world is one factor leading to major swings in usage of certain minerals. A worldwide recession, for example, will slow construction of new houses and buildings, and also slow demand for building materials. Copper demand for pipes and wires will therefore decline. Down goes the economy dependent on copper.

Technology can also change the demand for a particular mineral. The growth of catalytic converters spurred demand for platinum. Technological change can work in either direction. Mercury production has fallen by 75 percent as the world's developed countries have developed alternatives to mercury that are less toxic. Today, virtually all of the world's mercury mines have been closed. The demand that remains is filled through by-product mining (mercury is a by-product of zinc and gold mining) and through recycling.

Mineral supply can change, even though it tends to be more stable than demand. The discovery of gold in Alaska in 1896, for example, brought down the value of gold. In more recent years, development of new refining techniques brought another round of downward pressure on the yellow metal.

If you are a business manager selling products in a country dependent on one major product, you need to monitor that product. Step one is to determine just how important that product is to the country. Common talk may be helpful, but people tend to overplay the most visible elements of an economy. That is, folks in Seattle tend to overplay Boeing's role in that city, just as residents of Los Angeles overplay the entertainment industry. Thus, it will be useful to talk to someone who has gone over the statistics and really understands the country's sensitivity to the product.

Risk of a key commodity booming or collapsing can work either for a company or against it. If the company is primarily selling in the foreign country, then high prices for the key commodity are good, and low prices are bad. If you're trying to sell toothpaste in Ghana, then you're hoping for high cocoa prices. You also make contingency plans against low cocoa prices.

If, however, your organization is using Sri Lanka as a manufacturing location for something else—T-shirts, say— then commodity risk can have a surprisingly backward effect. That is, high tea prices are good for the country. The boom, however, can make labor hard to find. Workers may abandon factory work to go back to the tea industry. Transportation and other key services may be diverted to the booming sector. In short, the commodity boom may bid up the cost of labor and real estate.

Falling commodity prices may help the other manufacturers, of course. Labor and other services will be easier to secure. Remember, however, that this is not a permanent situation. The commodity price will probably bounce back, and workers will once again shift over to the more remunerative sector. The lesson here is to understand the underlying structure of the economy, rather than just react to current changes. Then the cycles can be used positively. For example, real estate will be cheap to acquire during the downside of the commodity cycle. Expansion plans should be deferred, if possible, in the upside of the cycle.

KEY POINT

Countries whose economy is dependent on one or two commodities are prone to boom-bust cycles caused by price fluctuation of those commodities.

TRADING PARTNER RISK

Small countries can be at substantial risk due to problems with their major trading partner. For example, Canada sells 85 percent of its exports to the United States. Canadian policymakers may be doing the best possible job, but if the United States goes into recession, Canada is certain to either turn down as well or enter a period of very sluggish growth. Trading partners that constitute risk to a country are typically nearby and are typically much larger economies. Canada is probably the most extreme case, though very small countries come close. About 80 percent of St. Lucia's banana exports go to the United Kingdom, and bananas are the country's major crop. More typical concentrations, though, show the largest trading partner buying 20 to 25 percent of a country's exports. A quick scan of a country's major export partners will identify this risk.

KEY POINT

A country that has a large concentration of its exports to one other country is at risk if the key trading partner goes into recession.

FOREIGN EXCHANGE RISK

Exchange rates between different currencies often fluctuate. Sometimes two currencies are pegged so that they don't fluctuate. Even then, there's a risk of the peg being moved. Foreign exchange rate fluctuations present challenges to companies with overseas operations.

Profits earned overseas may be translated into dollars at a higher or lower exchange rate. Even if the underlying business is earning steady profits in the local currency, the dollar profits that fall to the parent company's bottom line can be highly variable. To begin with, managers should understand what is happening, and any report of a foreign operation should clarify performance in both the foreign currency and the dollar. Next, corporations should consider hedging their foreign exchange risk using derivatives. Although derivatives can be very complex and highly dangerous, they can also be used to reduce risk. A good banker can help out on this issue.

Profit translation problems assume that there are profits. Swings in exchange rates can increase, decrease, and even eliminate the profits of overseas operations. For example, when the dollar is strong, it may appear profitable to set up an overseas manufacturing operation and then import the products. If the dollar declines in value, though, the dollars that U.S. customers pay for their products may not cover the manufacturing costs in the foreign country. As a result, proposals for overseas operations have to consider a wide variety of possible foreign exchange rates. When the overseas commitment is a substantial one, it has to be able to survive a significant adverse exchange rate movement.

Forecasts of exchange rates are notoriously unreliable. As a young forecaster, I carefully tracked my forecast accuracy. I did fairly well with GDP and inflation, somewhat well with interest rates, and worst of all with exchange rates. Academic research has found that Wall Street economists' forecasts of exchange rates are not better than a random number. For this reason, you should make sure that the success of an overseas venture does not depend on an accurate exchange rate forecast.

A final issue involves compensation of expatriate managers. Oftentimes some or all of an executive's salary is paid in the local currency. That's fine for renting local housing and buying local food. It doesn't work so well with saving for one's American retirement, putting one's children through an American university, or paying the mortgage on the American vacation home. Some mix of local and dollar pay is probably best, though it's unavoidable that some risk will be involved.

KEY POINTS

Exchange rate fluctuations can make overseas profits translate into more dollars or fewer dollars.	Exchange rate fluctuations can change the underlying profitability of overseas operations.

FINANCIAL CRISES IN FOREIGN COUNTRIES

Financial crises pose two risks to the business selling goods or services overseas. The first risk is foreign exchange controls, which can prevent movement of profits or capital from the foreign country. The second risk is that a financial crisis may cause a recession in the target market. A full explanation of financial crises is well beyond the scope of this book, but here are some things you should know as a manager in order to understand the basic risks and how to anticipate them.

A financial crisis occurs when a country no longer has the foreign exchange reserves or the credit that it needs to continue meeting its international obligations. Here's a fictional example that captures the essential elements. Ruritania is a small country whose currency is the ruro. The Central Bank of Ruritania pegs the ruro to the U.S. dollar at a ratio of three ruros per dollar. Now suppose that Ruritanian businesses, households, and investors are selling the ruro and buying dollars. Perhaps they need dollars to buy imported goods, or perhaps they want to buy investment securities in other countries because they are doubtful about the future value of the ruro. If Ruritania has a high inflation rate, its citizens may believe that dollars keep their value better than ruros. To keep the pegged exchange rate in the face of all this selling of ruros, the Ruritanian central bank purchases the ruros that everyone else is getting rid of, paying for them with U.S. dollars from its own account. Ruritania can do this for a while, say to weather a temporary loss of confidence. But it cannot continue paying out dollars indefinitely because it will run out of dollars. One possible resolution is to devalue the currency, changing the exchange rate between ruros and dollars to reflect the lesser demand for ruros.

Another type of crisis is a loss of credit. International banks may provide financing to Ruritanian banks or directly to Ruritanian businesses. If the international banks become nervous about the ability of Ruritanians to repay these debts, they may stop providing new credit and ask for repayment of all maturing loans. Ruritanian companies can no longer obtain credit from banks, neither their local banks nor international banks.

The possible results of these crises include devaluation, foreign exchange restrictions (also called capital controls), loss of domestic credit facilities, and recession.

Devaluation of the currency is a common result of a financial crisis. In 1994, Mexico had been pegging the peso to the dollar at a ratio of three pesos per greenback. The new president, Ernesto Zedillo, let the peso float—or, rather, sink. From one-third of a dollar it fell to a value of one-tenth of a buck. Mexicans call this *el error de diciembre*, the December mistake. For American companies overseas, their first problem was that a peso of earnings translated into fewer American dollars. The overseas manager who was hitting her numbers in pesos suddenly was not hitting her numbers in dollars. If the subsidiary had accumulated a large pile of pesos, there was an immediate loss of value to the hoard.

Foreign exchange restrictions prevent companies from shifting their local currency assets into dollars. Malaysia instituted such restrictions in 1997, early in the Asian financial crisis. Foreign exchange controls are government restrictions on the movement of money, typically out of the country.

The impact of foreign exchange controls can be severe. An American company may not be able to move profits earned overseas back home. The profits may still be kept in the foreign country and used to build the business, but they cannot be taken out to be redeployed in another country, to be paid out in dividends to American shareholders, or to be used to pay off debt held in the United States. The company may also be limited in its ability to buy capital goods or raw materials from vendors in other countries. Thus, profits might pile up, but if the company needs foreign-made capital goods in order to expand, it's stuck. There are sometimes exceptions made in order to keep businesses going. During Mexico's currency crisis, for example, *maquiladoras* (foreign-owned assembly plants) were given special dispensation. Some of these companies import basic components, say electronic parts from Asia. They assemble the parts into a finished product, then sell the goods to customers in the United States. Mexico realized that the operation generated more foreign exchange than it used. Therefore, the country would be better off relaxing the foreign exchange controls for importing goods so that they could be re-exported. No similar concessions were made, however, for Mexican consumers wanting to purchase imported goods.

The financial crisis often leads to a recession in the foreign country. The Indonesian financial crisis of 1998 showed how foreign exchange crises can lead to domestic recession. The manufacturing sector of Indonesia relied on bank credit for finance. Large companies would borrow from international banks, with their obligations in dollars. Smaller firms would borrow from local banks, which in turn had borrowed dollars from international banks. The credit supported the working capital needs of the country's manufacturers. The Asian financial crises led to a rethinking by Western lenders of the financial soundness of borrowers in Indonesia and elsewhere in Asia. Devaluation of the rupiah prevented large manufacturers from repaying their dollar-denominated loans to the large international banks. Indonesian banks, similarly, could not repay their dollar-denominated debt, and had to restrict credit to the small manufacturers they had previously lent to. Many of these manufacturing firms were profitable and could have continued to be profitable. They merely needed credit so that they could continue to purchase raw materials and pay wages until such time as their own accounts receivable were paid. There's good reason to be suspicious of a company that claims it wouldn't have gone bankrupt if it only had access to credit. However, it's a different story when the company has a history of access to credit which is suddenly terminated, and there are no other lenders willing and able to step into the breach.

The collapse of Indonesia's small manufacturing sector hurt the country. The sudden devaluation of the Indonesian currency caused prices of all imported goods to suddenly spike up. At the higher prices, Indonesian families had less purchasing power, further aggravating the recession.

The bottom line is that the foreign currency crisis didn't only affect banks and investment houses. It didn't only limit a company's ability to repatriate profits. It clobbered the ability of the country's people to buy goods and services. That's a significant risk to a business that was betting on the continuation of the local market.

KEY POINTS

Foreign exchange crises can wreck local businesses that were fundamentally sound.

Foreign exchange controls that limit a corporation's ability to move money around the world are often imposed during a crisis.

WAR AND REVOLUTION

Wars are not good for countries. This is especially true with regard to countries that get invaded. War may bring with it seizure of assets by the invading army. This may be a problem for the company selling in the country, but it means even more trouble for the company with production facilities. Factories tend to be more valuable spoils of war than stores or distribution centers—though anything can be seized by invading armies.

Recession or severe depression may envelope a country embroiled in war. The government's need for funds will lead to high taxes or inflation or both. The loss of purchasing power by the populace will make the country a poor marketing prospect, except for military supplies.

Finally, war may very well disrupt civilian supply chains. A factory or sales facility may be situated well away from the battle lines but nonetheless depend on supplies that have to cross the front. Some countries are victims of embargoes, which also squeeze supply chains. Similarly, damage to water or electricity plants may leave a factory without the means to continue operations.

Factory managers generally acknowledge infrastructure problems in less-developed countries. Plants are more likely to need backup generators, for example, in countries with less-reliable electric utility systems. Add the potential for war-time disruption of the electrical grid to the list of reasons for backup power.

Revolution may have all of the effects of war, only spread out widely across the country. It is also possible, though, for a country to have a coup d'etat that has minimal impact on business. Assassinations are, in some countries, more common than orderly changes in power. The business operating in a less-stable country must consider how closely its fortunes are tied to the ruling regime. If the company needed special licenses or concessions from the government, then the entire venture is at risk from a change of regime.

Companies that have substantial fixed assets are also at risk from revolutions and coups. If the company doesn't like the new regime, it cannot very well quit the game and take its ball home. The new regime may seize the company's assets. More likely, it can impose high taxes that effectively seize the asset but leave enough on the table that the company continues to operate. It may never earn enough to recoup its fixed investment, but it may earn more than if it had just walked away in disgust. Because of these risks, large fixed investments work better in stable countries than in less-stable countries.

In general, signs of revolution should be considered red flags for businesses, whether they are producing or selling in the country.

KEY POINT

Wars, coups d'etat, and assassinations pose serious risks to companies operating overseas. Thus, political stability must be evaluated carefully before making large foreign investments.

MANAGING THROUGH THE FOREIGN BUSINESS CYCLE

Business strategy in a foreign recession depends entirely on the nature of the business activity. If the overseas operation is selling into the local market (for instance, Procter and

Gamble selling toothpaste in Thailand), the standard strategy steps for dealing with a recession will apply, though with a few changes. However, if the foreign activity is primarily production (Intel manufacturing computer chips overseas), then different issues emerge.

In the case of a business selling to residents of the foreign country, there are a couple of twists to consider. Staffing levels in many developed countries cannot be adjusted as easily as they can in the United States. Layoffs may be prohibited, or they may be so expensive in terms of severance benefits that little money is saved.

Less-developed countries may have less-developed markets for factoring (the selling of accounts receivable). A business that extends a fair amount of trade credit in a foreign country should investigate the local factoring capability. Even if the company expects that it will not sell its receivables, knowing whether or not they *could* be sold is important. If a recession may put pressure on cash flow, then getting to know the local factors is important and should be done well before they are needed.

A business that is producing goods overseas for sale in the American market has a different set of problems than a business selling to the local market. Sales levels will not be affected by the foreign recession, so all appears fine at first. However, local vendors may be in trouble. If your factory accounts for 10 percent of a vendor's business, you may not be able to keep him afloat in a recession. Other vendors will no doubt be happy to take his place, but changing vendors can cause business disruption, especially for customized products. Buyers for the American company should get to know their vendors. They may want to see financial statements for critical vendors. They certainly want to get to know the vendor well enough that they understand his business. If the vendor's sales are primarily to expatriate manufacturers, then there shouldn't be big worries. But vendors who are mostly selling to locally owned businesses may be at risk of bankruptcy. Even if they don't go bankrupt, they may lack working capital to continue operations.

During the Asian financial crisis of 1997–1998, a number of Southeast Asian companies that were fundamentally sound went into bankruptcy because they could not meet their dollar-denominated debt payments. They were "fundamentally sound" in the sense that they could convert raw materials into finished goods at a reasonable profit margin. However, they were bankrupt because the value of their debt had skyrocketed, not through excessive borrowing but because their local currency had fallen relative to the dollar. American businesses dependent on these bankrupt vendors had three choices. First, they could find another vendor. For common goods and services, plenty of other vendors were around. The second choice was to buy the vendor. Many owners of foreign companies would have gladly sold their businesses for the value of their debt. Even better for the American purchaser would be to buy the company from its debtors, at cents on the dollar. The former owner was usually still around to run the operation, provided the right incentive plan was in effect. The third option to the American company was to provide financing to its vendors. Sometimes this seems like a good, simple solution.

For instance, the American business could prepay for the goods it needed to buy, thereby providing the vendor with working capital to purchase raw materials and to keep

"Vendors who are mostly selling to locally owned businesses may be at risk of bankruptcy."

workers on the job. However, prepayment did not guarantee that the vendor would not go bankrupt before the goods were delivered. If that happened, the American business would have nothing to show for trying to work with its vendors. A slightly safer version of this strategy would be to buy the raw materials and have them delivered to the vendor's factory. If the legal system is solid, the vendor would get its raw materials back in a bankruptcy. Unfortunately, many of the countries prone to such financial crises do not have well-developed legal institutions, and the inventory could be tied up in corrupt courts for years.

The best strategy is based on knowing one's vendors and knowing alternative vendors. Only when the supply chain is truly in danger should other options, such as buying a company, be implemented.

When the economy is improving, overseas managers should worry about whether vendors will uphold preexisting price agreements. For instance, suppose that in the depths of a foreign recession, you contract with a local company to buy cardboard boxes for $1 per box. You are going to need 1 million boxes a year, and you sign a contract that sets the quantity and price for three years. In some countries, that contract will not be honored after the economy recovers. If, after recovery, the vendor can sell his boxes to someone else for $1.15 each, you are out of luck. The more developed the country, the greater the likelihood that the courts would take your side in the dispute. Many countries, however, have only crude systems for adjudicating contracts. The lesson? Be wary of good multiyear deals. It's better to take low pricing in the recession and to pay through the nose in the boom than to pay moderate prices in the recession and then have to pay through the nose.

KEY POINTS		
Business strategy for a foreign recession varies depending on whether the company is selling to the local market or using the foreign country to produce goods for the home market.	A recession strategy for firms selling to the foreign market should be much like one for dealing with a U.S. downturn.	A recession strategy for firms producing overseas for the home market should focus on ascertaining the viability of local suppliers and using the downturn to secure good deals.

THE MONITORING SYSTEM

The management function of a business operating in a foreign country may partially be conducted in the home country. That is, a corporate manager in the United States may oversee the company's operations in Chile. Somewhere, either at home or abroad, a monitoring system needs to be established.

The monitoring system begins as it would for operations in the United States. Monetary policy is watched; the potential for an oil price hike is periodically evaluated; secondary factors such as waves of optimism and pessimism are watched; swings in government spending are considered. In the foreign country, though, the monitoring system needs some adjustment.

For a major industrialized country (such as Japan, Australia, Canada, or major European countries), the monitoring system would closely resemble that used in the United States. The particulars of monetary policy would be somewhat different, especially in countries that use the euro as their currency. The positive side of the euro is that one set of information about monetary policy covers all of the countries that use the euro.

In less-developed countries, more information is needed about the structure of monetary policy before a specific data collection system can be put into place. How is monetary policy conducted? What are the key indicators of policy? The yield curve is a good indicator in the United States, but in some countries the market for government debt is not as well developed. Thus, the spread between short-term and long-term interest rates on government bonds may show more noise than signal. As a result, the measures used to evaluate the stance of monetary policy will vary from country to country.

Closely associated with monetary policy is the risk of a foreign exchange crisis. The foreign exchange rate may sometimes be stable but unsustainable. That is, the country is trying to maintain an exchange rate that is inconsistent with economic fundamentals. The current stability of the exchange rate masks the decreasing prospects for continuing that exchange rate.

BUSINOMICS JARGON MADE CLEAR: *PURCHASING POWER PARITY*

▶ This term refers to an exchange rate at which two different currencies buy the same amount of goods in their two countries. If it takes $3 to buy a bushel of wheat in the United States, and twelve pesos to buy a bushel in Mexico, then an exchange ratio of four-to-one is purchasing power parity. You can spend $3 to buy the bushel in the United States, or you can convert your $3 into twelve pesos and buy a bushel of wheat in Mexico.

How can the business manager watch for this possibility? Some of the major investment banks publish estimates of purchasing power parity. Purchasing power parity means that one currency should be able to buy as much stuff as another currency. Exchange rates don't always match purchasing power parity, but over time, relative price levels in the two countries do influence exchange rates.

Small differences—5 to 10 percent—can be continued for some time. Larger differences, especially if they are increasing, suggest that something will have to give. Either monetary policy has to change to bring the rates of inflation in the two countries in line, or the exchange rate needs to adjust to reflect the differing purchase powers. The bottom line for business managers is simple: Find estimates of purchasing power parity exchange rates, and watch for large and growing divergences.

Countries that are receiving a substantial amount of foreign investment can grow faster because of the capital inflow, but they are also more vulnerable to disruptions of the inflow. A country can become dependent on growth. This is evidenced by a large construction sector and by substantial resources being put into capital spending. The mood of international investors should be monitored. Drops in the country's stock exchange prices and lowered bond credit ratings are indicators of problems.

Oil supply shocks can be monitored in a foreign country much as they are monitored in the United States, with the proviso that the country will be more or less dependent on foreign oil than the United States. Thus, the effect on the country of a large swing in oil prices may be greater or lesser than we are used to. The monitoring is the same, only the impact of the gauge is different.

Commodity price risk is fairly simple to measure. If the country is dependent on coffee for a major portion of its economy, then one looks at coffee prices. We're talking wholesale bean prices, of course, not Starbucks retail price lists.

Trading partner risk is fairly easy to watch. A schedule of the country's export destinations is examined. If there are one or two major trading partners that put the country at risk, then those will stand out. Most of these lists are based on merchandise exports, but in some cases tourism must be added. For instance, Greece's large tourism economy adds to its dependence on Germany beyond what would be suggested by a listing of Greece's exports of goods.

Once the major trading partner is identified, then it is monitored the same way that any other country is monitored.

The risk of war or internal rebellion is best monitored through the local and international press. The local press needs to be supplemented by other sources if the government controls the media tightly. In countries with vigorous and independent newspapers, the local newspaper may suffice.

Setting up a monitoring system for a foreign country is not always easy, but the manager who reviews the economic data gains a better understanding of the country by doing so. If, however, a manager in America is responsible for operations in thirty countries, he or she obviously needs some help. Staff support for the monitoring system is possible. Another option is to subscribe to a service that provides regular information about the countries of interest. This may be available from an investment bank (at no charge to its clients) or from a media company such as the *Economist*, which offers a number of supplemental country and industry reports in addition to its excellent magazine.

Another monitoring option that should be considered is engaging a local economist to provide regular reports. Not just any economist will do, of course. It's necessary to have one who is not philosophically opposed to business. The economist must also be one who watches current business and political events, rather than sticking with theory or researching obscure subjects that don't have application to your business.

KEY POINTS		
An early warning system should be established for every foreign country of importance to your company.	Early warning systems for developed countries will resemble a U.S. early warning system, with foreign exchange risk added.	In less-developed countries, the system must also include the potential for foreign exchange crisis, war and political upheaval, commodity risk, and trading partner risks.

CONTINGENCY PLANS

After the monitoring system is in place, contingency plans need to be sketched out. As was discussed in Chapter 5, these should not be detailed plans bound to catch dust. However, the executive in charge needs to give some serious consideration to the company's risks and options for dealing with difficulties.

The specifics of the contingency plans depend upon the risks present. Every country faces some risk of recession. The basics of how to deal with a recession are consistent across countries, so the manager should consult the discussion of this topic in Chapter 7.

Some countries, however, face economic risks other than recession. To begin with, foreign exchange crises can limit movement of capital out of the foreign country. Some countries, such as China, have foreign exchange controls as a permanent feature of the regulatory environment. Other countries, such as Mexico in the 1980s, have instituted controls in reaction to a crisis. This risk caused by foreign exchange controls can be mitigated ahead of time by keeping capital lean within the foreign country.

For example, if the company needs to borrow money for its foreign operations, it should consider borrowing in the foreign country, perhaps guaranteed by the parent company. Repayment of that debt is then a financial transaction within the country. If foreign exchange controls are imposed, the company will be able to repay its debt because it does not need to move cash internationally to do so. Suppose, in contrast, that the parent company borrowed money in the United States and then moved the capital into the foreign country. The country gets into foreign exchange trouble and forbids the movement of hard currency outside the country. Now our company is in trouble, even if it is fundamentally profitable. It cannot move money back to the United States to repay the debt. This company may have to default on its debt just because it cannot move its own funds around the world.

Once the risk is recognized, there will be a number of ways identified to mitigate the risk. A good bank's foreign exchange desk should be able to help develop such strategies, but in general, the company has to realize that it needs help.

Small-country commodity risk is not easily mitigated. For companies selling in the foreign country, sales are sure to decline. Being prepared for the usual steps to take in a downturn is all a manager can do. For companies with production facilities in a small country with commodity risk, the danger is the boom in the commodity pulling labor and other resources away from the nonbooming sectors. The best strategy is, as usual, to plan ahead. Let the workers know that your firm is a stable employer that will keep them on staff even during down markets but that you may not be hiring after the commodity boom is over. Make sure that your real estate, raw materials supply, and transportation arrangements are in solid, long-term contracts.

War and revolution present a substantial challenge. When the risk of either becomes apparent, a company's first concern should be the safety of its employees. Evacuations may be called for, though if they prove to be unnecessary, the business is likely to suffer from the absence of repatriated employees.

The next risk from war and revolution is asset seizure, but there is little to be done in the face of an invading army. More common than outright seizure, and easier to manage, is loss of utilities and transportation. Thus, contingency plans for war and revolution should entail how to deal with cutoffs of electricity, oil or natural gas, and water. Key inputs may not be delivered to the plant, so stockpiles might be accumulated ahead of time (especially if the risk of asset seizure is considered low). Similarly, storage of finished products may become an issue if transport is temporarily unavailable.

For the company selling into a country at war, expect to experience weak consumer and business demand for discretionary projects. Families will be hoarding their liquid assets, and businesses will be uncertain whether capital expansion projects should be continued. There will be a market for military supplies and related items, such as field rations and fuel oil. Generally, though, sales in a country at war will stink.

Businesses can gain in a foreign cycle, just as they can in a domestic recession. Ayala Group, a Philippine conglomerate, came out of the Asian financial crisis smelling like a rose. In 1996, before the problems began, Ayala had very little debt and a large supply of cash. The following years, Philippine companies cancelled their capital expenditures, and many companies went bankrupt. Ayala's subsidiary Globe Telecom, in contrast, continued its build-out of a new digital wireless network. Globe Telecom is now the largest cell phone company in the country. Ayala's banking subsidiary bought out one of its largest competitors, jumping from the fifth-largest bank to the second-largest in one fell swoop. The key to Ayala's success during the Philippines recession is straightforward. They had low debt and much cash before the recession, and they were not afraid to spend cash and borrow more in order to take advantage of the opportunities that arose during the downturn.

KEY POINTS

Contingency plans for a foreign recession should include the common elements of a domestic plan, plus plans for the various exchange rate and capital flow risks.

Plans for alternative supply chains should be in place, including utility service.

SUMMING UP

Economic fluctuations are more varied in certain foreign countries, especially less-developed countries. They present a much larger challenge to the manager trying to monitor developments and assess risk. The set of actions that may be needed to deal with the risks are far wider than what a general manager in the United States usually needs to be concerned with. One approach that managers may want to consider is diversifying their international operations. For sales-oriented companies, it's easy enough to sell in a number of countries. Production-oriented companies should consider having offshore facilities in very different regions, such as one in Asia, one in Latin America, and one in Eastern Europe.

This listing of risks is not evidence that foreign business should be shunned. Doing business abroad can be quite profitable, but only if the economic risks are understood, monitored, and planned for.

BUSINOMICS

Regional Economic Cycles: Your Local Economy

WILLIAM B. CONERLY, PH.D.—A region of the country will tend to move up and down with the national economy, but it will not be perfectly synchronized to the national economy. The business executive whose operations are contained in a distinct region of the country needs to monitor the national economy. This need cannot be ignored by large companies serving the national market. Although the CEO of a national restaurant chain doesn't have to worry about how Peoria is doing, the regional manager for Peoria certainly should be focused on the local economy. Furthermore, corporate analysts assessing the quality of their managers need to consider the underlying economy in each of their regions. Basically, the broader national economy will affect a state's economy, but the economic situation in a state will also be influenced by the national cycle for its most important industries and by its own internal growth cycle.

Most of this chapter takes the perspective of a business executive selling into a distinct local market. In one section, "Production in a Regional Economy" (page 213), we'll discuss issues specific to companies whose operations are primarily production rather than sales. For example, the biotech company located in Boston is probably selling into a national or global market and can ignore the regional economy as a sales market. However, this business must consider the regional economic cycle's impacts on local labor and real estate markets.

In the remainder of this chapter, we'll discuss regional economics in terms of states. However, the same analysis can be applied to groups of states, a metropolitan area, or a group of metropolitan areas. The analysis can also be applied to a county or group of counties. However, the necessary data may not be available for counties or smaller metropolitan areas.

The national economy will almost always be the largest single driver of the regional economy. However, every region has swings that are distinctive. States or metropolitan areas will have downturns that are more or less severe than the national cycle, primarily because of the structure of regional production. For instance, the San Jose metropolitan area, which comprises Silicon Valley, enjoyed 6 percent employment growth in 2000, which was significantly faster than the national average. Then the high-tech sector collapsed. In 2002, San Jose lost 10 percent of its jobs, far worse than the national average.

In addition to being sensitive to national industrial cycles, states can have their own cycles associated with construction swings.

REGIONAL PRODUCTION STRUCTURE

The business manager assessing risk of regional recession should first begin by determining how similar the region is to the national economy. A similarity index measures how closely each state's major categories of earnings match the national pattern. If a state perfectly reflected the national distribution of earnings by sector, its index value would be 100. High values are more like the nation; lower values are less like the nation. (Similarity indexes are prepared by the U.S. Bureau of Economic Analysis; a link is available at *www.businomics.com*.)

TABLE 9-A

Most Similar States	Similarity Index	Least Similar States	Similarity Index
California	88.4	Mississippi	65.1
Georgia	87.5	West Virginia	64.7
Missouri	87.4	North Dakota	64.6
Illinois	86.3	New Mexico	63.0
New Jersey	85.3	Montana	59.3
Pennsylvania	84.7	Nevada	54.4
Texas	84.5	Hawaii	52.7
Utah	84.4	Alaska	44.6
Washington	84.4	Wyoming	42.8
Rhode Island	82.9	District of Columbia	9.9

The top states are very similar to the national economy. A business that sells to the California market will find that its sales fluctuate primarily with the national business cycle. On the other hand, Wyoming is very unlike the nation. Companies doing business there should drill down to understand the major industry (which happens to be mining, with a secondary emphasis on government services).

TABLE 9-B

State	Similarity Index	State	Similarity Index
Alabama	77.7	Montana	59.3
Alaska	44.6	Nebraska	79.1
Arizona	82.7	Nevada	54.4
Arkansas	70.2	New Hampshire	77.0
California	88.4	New Jersey	85.3
Colorado	77.3	New Mexico	63.0
Connecticut	74.7	New York	67.8
Delaware	76.6	North Carolina	82.7
District of Columbia	9.9	North Dakota	64.6
Florida	78.7	Ohio	79.8
Georgia	87.5	Oklahoma	72.4
Hawaii	52.7	Oregon	82.2
Idaho	79.3	Pennsylvania	84.7
Illinois	86.3	Rhode Island	82.9
Indiana	68.6	South Carolina	71.8
Iowa	75.5	South Dakota	69.1
Kansas	81.5	Tennessee	75.8
Kentucky	73.1	Texas	84.5
Louisiana	76.4	Utah	84.4
Maine	75.7	Vermont	73.1
Maryland	73.7	Virginia	69.9
Massachusetts	75.6	Washington	84.4
Michigan	75.1	West Virginia	64.7
Minnesota	82.4	Wisconsin	74.8
Mississippi	65.1	Wyoming	42.8
Missouri	87.4		

For states or regions with high similarity, the national economy will be the largest driver of economic cycles. States with a low similarity will display cycles that vary more from the national pattern. Chart 9.1 illustrates that California, with its high similarity, moves closely with the national economy. Wyoming, the least similar state, has some similarities and some differences. Since 1990, Wyoming has moved up and down roughly in parallel with the United States. But the 1970s and 1980s were a very different story. The explanation underlying this pattern is Wyoming's concentration in the mining industry (which includes oil and gas production as well as traditional mining, such as coal). Wyoming boomed when energy prices were rising, but the state's economy then dropped sharply when energy prices fell. Anyone doing business in Wyoming should have been aware that Wyoming could move very differently than the national economy.

Details on how to calculate similarity indexes appear in the appendix.

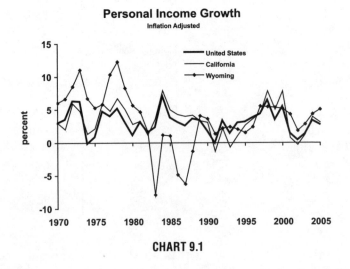

CHART 9.1

State-level measures may not be appropriate for all businesses, however. A restaurant supplier in California's Silicon Valley will have a very different experience than a similar company in Los Angeles.

Having established a state's similarity with the national economy, it's now time to determine which industries are the major drivers of the economy. Most of us have a rough idea of our region's major industries. Surprisingly, many of us are wrong. The most common error is to overestimate the importance of the major industries. Newspaper headlines tend to emphasize the largest, most visible companies, but they often miss the many small companies that, in the aggregate, have a substantial impact. Californians will sometimes speak as if their state moves up or down with aerospace and high tech. However, as its similarity index shows, California seldom diverges too much from the national cycle. Although major industries are often overemphasized, they sometimes are underrecognized. For example, in my discussions with business leaders in the Tacoma, Washington, area, it's clear that they see the military as a significant, but not the most significant, factor in the regional economy. The data, however, indicate that the area's two major military bases have a huge influence on the regional economy.

Determining a state or region's key industries is a fairly easy statistical exercise. Our goal is to determine a "location quotient" for each industry. A location quotient is a measure that shows the importance of an industry to a state or metropolitan area relative to that industry's importance to the national economy.

We begin with basic data. As an example, we'll look at farm earnings in Kansas, as shown in the table below. The columns "Percentage of total" show farm earnings as a percentage of earnings by place of work (which is total earnings for our purposes). This tells us that in the United States as a whole, farm earnings are 0.81 percent of total earnings, or just under 1 percent. In Kansas, though, farms contribute

1.42 percent of earnings. The location quotient is computed as 1.42 percent divided by 0.81 percent, or 1.75. Any location quotient over 1 indicates that the industry is more important to the state economy than it is to the national economy.

TABLE 9-C

	United States	Percentage of Total	Kansas	Percentage of Total	Location Quotient	Dollar Difference
Earnings by Place of Work*	$7,566,609		$65,154			
Farm Earnings*	$61,175	0.81%	$922	1.42%	1.75	$395

Note: Dollar values in Table 9-C are expressed in millions

However, it doesn't make sense to simply look at industries with high location quotients. There may be a very tiny sector that is more important in a particular state. Even though it has a high location quotient, it's still pretty tiny. For example, if you told me that Oklahoma has a horseshoe industry that is twice the size, on a percentage basis, as the national horseshoe industry, I'd still say "So what?" But if you made the same statement about a larger sector, such as the military, then we'd have an important sector to watch.

What we want is a measure that looks at both how big the difference for the state is, and also how big the industry is. For that reason, I like to translate the location quotient into a dollar difference. The idea of the dollar difference is how much bigger the industry is in dollar terms. We begin by calculating what Kansas farm earnings would have been if farming were exactly as important in Kansas as in the country as a whole. That is, we multiply the Kansas income of $65 billion by the U.S. farm earnings percentage, which is

0.81 percent. That gives us $527 million. We subtract this from Kansas's actual farm earnings of $922 million to arrive at a dollar difference of $395 million. (I haven't rounded my figures, so you will arrive at a slightly different calculation if you check my work with your calculator.) The economic interpretation of the dollar difference is how much bigger Kansas's earnings are because its farm sector is larger than the national average. (Data for these calculations are from the U.S. Bureau of Economic Analysis's report on state personal income. A link is provided on *www.businomics.com*.)

After doing a similar calculation for all industries, Kansas's major concentrations have been identified: transportation equipment manufacturing, food processing, military, and farming. (Those who wonder about transportation equipment should look at Wichita's many aircraft factories.)

At this step, the regional manager knows how much her state varies from the national economy and which industries will have a greater weight in the state or region. The final step is to consider whether nearby states should also be considered. Connecticut, for example, is highly correlated with economic activity in New York City. There are a number of cities included in the metropolitan areas of a different state, such as Overland Park, Kansas, which is just outside of Kansas City, Missouri, or Vancouver, Washington, just across the Columbia River from Portland, Oregon. It may be necessary to look at neighboring states to understand a region's economy.

At this stage, we know how to determine a state's sensitivity to the national economic cycle, and we know how to determine which industries are most important to the state. Understanding the state's economy now consists of understanding the national economy overall, plus the particular industries that are more important to the state. Those industries, and thus the state economy, will follow the economic patterns described in Chapter 2 with regard to degree of cyclicality, trend growth, and the timing of cycles.

Regions can have growth cycles that are driven through the state's own dynamics, which is the subject of the next section. However, through the overall economy and through the industries that are concentrated in the state, national impacts will almost always play a much greater role than economic forces that are wholly internal to the state.

KEY POINTS

The overall national economy usually has a greater effect on a region than any other factor.	The composition of a region's output, in conjunction with the composition of national economic growth, is the next greatest factor on a region's economic performance.

INTERNAL REGIONAL CYCLES

The factors that cause business cycles usually operate across all of the regions of a country. Monetary policy, oil shocks, waves of optimism, and pessimism generally impact very broad swathes of the country or the world. However, some local cycles can be caused by variations in regional growth.

The largest driver of internal cycles is population growth. When an area develops a reputation for being a great place to live, people tend to move in. The migration into a region triggers the need for new houses, new stores, new offices, and so forth. Construction booms. This construction is the key to understanding internal regional cycles.

▶ The focus of this book is short-term economic fluctuations, but many business and civic leaders wonder what makes a region grow over a decade or an even longer time span. There are two basic answers to the question, which I call the Alaska answer and the Arizona answer.

The Alaska answer is that jobs attract people. The history of that state, and of others as well, is that population flowed in when there was good work: mining gold, building defense facilities, or constructing the oil pipeline. In between the major projects, people tended to leave.

The Alaska answer certainly applies in some cases, at some times, but it has been supplanted in usefulness by the Arizona answer: People move for quality of life, and the jobs follow. Most of the work done in Arizona could be done elsewhere in the country. The state is big in financial services, such as call centers for banks. Their manufacturing includes a fair number of high-tech facilities that are not tied to Arizona's resources. The explanation is that people came because they wanted

to live in Arizona. Then businesses expanded to take advantage of the population. People were willing to work a little cheaper because they loved living there. This has spawned the "second paycheck" theory of wages. If I live in a nice place, I get two paychecks. One is denominated in dollars and comes from my employer. The second paycheck is denominated in "quality of life" and makes up for the first paycheck being a little small. But the fact that I'll take some of my pay in quality of life makes me an attractive employee. Some businesses move in from out of state to take advantage of the available workforce, while other local businesses are able to expand and beat out-of-state competition because of their labor cost advantage.

The Arizona answer is now the dominant explanation for long-term growth in regions of the United States, though Alaska answers pop up here and there, depending on special local circumstances.

A small amount of construction merely replaces current housing and commercial buildings. Some houses burn down or are demolished or become so outdated that they are abandoned. New construction replaces these properties. However, most new construction is for growth. More people live in an area, and they need housing, places to work, places to shop in, doctors with offices, and so on. So a small amount of construction is proportional to the existing population, but most construction is proportional to the increase in population. (Readers who remember their college economics will recognize this concept as the "multiplier-accelerator" theory.)

Let's say that a state's population has been growing rapidly. Its construction sector will be booming, building all the new homes, stores, and offices needed because of the population increases. Now, after some time, let's say that population growth slows from 5 percent down to 3 percent. To put these figures in perspective, the natural increase in population (births minus deaths) runs at just over one-half percent of population in the United States. So population growth of 5 percent implies that many more people are moving in than moving out. The state is a magnet for footloose people.

What happens to this state when population growth drops from 5 percent to 3 percent? Three percent is still very strong, well above the national average. But the number of new homes needed is much lower. When the population growth is translated into housing needs, slower *growth* of population results in a decline in the *number* of new houses built. Moving from 5 percent growth to 3 percent growth implies a roughly 40 percent decline in the need for new housing. That, in turn, means a massive drop-off in construction employment. A state that is growing rapidly has risk that other states don't have, due to a potential decline in population growth.

Idaho in 1986 typified this kind of pattern. The state's population had been growing rapidly, around 3 percent per year, in the 1970s. Growth began to decline in the 1980s, and construction employment fell from over 19,000 to just over 13,000. In other words, construction activity fell by one-third as population growth slowed. This pulled total employment down by 2 percent, just from construction alone, before any ripple effects were considered.

The fast-growing state has other advantages, however. Faster-growing states tend to have more stable growth rates, which is a bit counterintuitive at first. The logic, though, is that every state's growth is a combination of stimulus from the national economy, based on the state's similarity and key industries, plus the state's own long-term growth trend. When that long-term growth trend plays a larger role, the national economy, with all of its cycles, plays a smaller role. It turns out that states' own growth cycles tend to be more stable than the national economy. Thus, places like Arizona and Nevada have more stable economies than slow-growing states.

KEY POINT

Changes in a region's population growth rate can cause
the state's economy to accelerate or decelerate.

ECONOMIC POLICY

One issue that can often be ignored in regional economic cycles is economic policy. In a downturn, every governor announces a plan to get the economy going. After the economy recovers, the governor takes credit for having created thousands of jobs. Most voters ignore this talk, and quite wisely.

State or local economic policy cannot change any of the big factors behind business cycles. They can provide some fiscal stimulus, such as through highway projects. However, even old-fashioned Keynesians acknowledge that state or local public works projects have less impact than national government spending. Much of the supposedly stimulative spending leaks out of the regional economy. In a typical public-works project, much of the materials are purchased from outside the region. These may include steel, cement, and lumber. The engineering work may be contracted to a firm outside the region. The actual workers on the project may be itinerant construction tradesmen, who move from project to project. Certainly a number of local residents will work on a large project, but the economic impact is reduced by various leakages.

Public works projects usually suffer from poor timing, as we discussed in Chapter 3. It takes months for lawmakers and the public to recognize that a recession has begun, then additional months to pass legislation, which often requires a bond levy for large projects. By the time the project begins, the recession is usually over.

Tax cuts to stimulate a state or local economy are common responses to a recession, but they seldom work very well. Most of the spending triggered by the tax cuts leak outside the local economy. Most consumer spending is on products made outside the consumer's local area, so the tax cut ends up stimulating some other region.

As a general rule, then, expect a local recession to resist the government's efforts to buck up the economy.

KEY POINT

State or local economic policy has little effect in the short run.

PRODUCTION IN A REGIONAL ECONOMY

Economic cycles have a different impact on the producer than on the seller. A business selling goods in a particular region will suffer when the area goes into recession. The business that only produces goods in the region will benefit from a local recession.

BUSINOMICS ECONOMIC POLICY FOR GROWTH

▶ Although economic policy cannot help a region deal with a business cycle, policy is important to long-term growth. That is, don't expect good policy to reverse a recession, but expect it to add a small amount to annual growth rates, year after year after year. That small amount compounds until an area with good policy will have grown noticeably compared to areas with poor policy.

Good tax policy involves either no state income tax or a tax at low marginal rate. (The marginal rate is the tax on an additional dollar of income.) There is substantial evidence that people are moving into states that do not have state income taxes. My own research has found faster economic growth in states with lower income tax rates.

The other important policy direction is an easy-to-navigate regulatory system. Businesses should be able to form, locate their operations, hire their employees, and engage in their transactions without navigating a bewildering and uncertain maze of regulations. The key here is transparency. The regulations that a state or local government want should be clear and easy to comply with. Regulations that are uncertain and that require many months for decisions are harmful to growth.

The usual economic development policy ideas, such as tax credits for companies moving in, are not effective. They cost the existing taxpayers more than the benefit they provide.

Producers, in this sense, include factories that manufacture goods that are predominantly sold outside the region in which they are produced. Think Detroit automakers. Developers of creative property also fall into this category. Think Microsoft in Seattle or Disney in Los Angeles. Call centers and financial processing facilities are also producers in this regard. Think of the credit card issuers in Wilmington, Delaware, or Sioux Falls, South Dakota.

Every company competes against every other business, nonprofit organization, and government agency for labor, land, and other productive resources. A cyclical downturn enables the producer to hire talented workers at a lower wage and to buy or lease buildings at a lower cost. Local vendors are likely to offer better pricing in a downturn. For instance, the local printers may do most of their business producing brochures and catalogs for local businesses. In a downturn, the producer company can get its employee handbook printed locally at a lower cost than it could when the economy was humming.

Strength in the local economy is uncomfortable for producers located there. Labor cost and availability suffers when workers have plentiful job opportunities at both local businesses and the national producers. In short, the impact of an economic cycle is just reversed for a producer selling into a national market, assuming that the national market is not affected by the same factors that impacted the local economy. For the producer, then, the analysis of the local economy is similar to a company selling in the local market, except that the direction of impact is reversed.

How often does one part of the country suffer when the rest of the country is strong? We emphasized earlier in this chapter that most areas are highly correlated with the national economy. However, there are always exceptions. Call to mind a few of the phrases that have been used in recent decades, such as rust belt, or bicoastal recession. The best bet is that a state mimics the national economy, but that bet sometimes loses. Hawaii suffered four years of declining employment in the mid-1990s even though the national economy grew steadily. The problem was that Japan had entered a severe recession, which reduced tourist spending in Hawaii. In 1985–1986, oil-producing states such as Louisiana and Oklahoma suffered while the national economy grew at a decent pace. In short, it's possible for a state or region to move counter to the national economy, though that's not usually the case.

KEY POINT

Regional producers benefit from weak local conditions,
and they are hurt by local economic strength.

A REGIONAL EARLY WARNING SYSTEM

The early warning system for a business operating in a particular region resembles the system described in Chapter 6. The national indicators are just as important for a regional business as they are for a national company. In addition, measures of the regional economy must be added. Begin with an identification of the key industries for the region. Then monitor those industries as one would monitor any industry. For example, a car dealer in the Washington, D.C., suburbs would monitor his own industry, automobile sales. In addition, he would monitor federal government activity, the key industry for his region. He monitors federal spending even if he sells no cars at all to the government. His customers work for the government, or they earn their livelihood from people who do work for the government. Thus, being a regional business adds to the number of industries that must be monitored in an early warning system.

In addition to national data on industries, a regional early warning system must watch local economic data. The best indicator to watch is nonfarm employment. The label "nonfarm" helps to define the dataset to watch. It's not that one takes total employment and subtracts out farm labor. Rather, the dataset that is most useful does not include farm labor, for various reporting reasons, so it's called nonfarm employment. These data are available for states, metropolitan areas, and, in most cases, counties. The data come out fairly promptly. The government reports other data candidates, such as gross state product and personal income, with a long time lag, so that they are useless as indicators of current economic activity. The nonfarm employment data are fairly accurate, though not perfect.

The unemployment rate is less useful, though often watched. Unemployment is measured in a telephone survey (not through filings for unemployment insurance claims, as is commonly thought). The survey results can be misleading due to discouraged people. To be counted as unemployed, one must be looking for work. As people get discouraged about the prospects of finding a job, they stop looking for work and are no longer counted as unemployed. Conversely, when job prospects improve, a number of people who had been discouraged start looking for work again. This increases unemployment, because now more people who are out of work report that they are looking for work. Thus, the unemployment rate is not a highly useful measure of the economy. Add to this the usual problems with telephone surveys, and it's easy to see why most economists make this indicator a low priority.

Personal income is a common measure of state economies, but it is published with about a three-month time lag. In addition, the first estimate that is published is frequently revised radically in later estimates. Thus, the first reliable estimate comes out six months late. As a result, this indicator is most useful for historical research, not for tracking the current economy.

State government revenue provides another look at the economy, especially for states that publish monthly updates. The best measure to use in monitoring the economy is withholding, though keep in mind that end-of-year data may be influenced by bonuses. Total tax collections are usually hard to interpret because they consist of many different taxes, as well as different types of collections for the income tax. The income tax may have withholding payments, estimated tax payments, regular payments or refunds with the tax return, and late payments.

"Personal income is a common measure of state economies, but it is published with about a three-month time lag."

Businesses in construction or other services for new residents should monitor permits for residential construction. The most common measure is the number of housing units permitted. In this definition, a duplex counts as two units, even though it's just one building.

Many state drivers-license bureaus can help a business monitor population flows. The bureaus report the number of licenses turned in by out-of-state residents who have come into the office to get a new driver's license. They also report the number of in-state licenses turned in to other state licensing agencies by people who have moved out. The difference between these two figures is net migration of drivers. The timing of these data series is not perfect. Typically, state departments of motor vehicles don't think of themselves as statistical collection agencies because that's not their primary responsibility. As a result, they may be casual about when they collect licenses and send them in to the statistics office. One month's figure may be unusually low, just because a few offices didn't report by month's end. Then the following month's figure is unusually high because it covers two months of data. With that caution, the figures do show trends pretty well. Most of the time it's best to take a twelve-month average, to account for both seasonality and some sloppiness in data collection.

Sales tax data, in those states with sales taxes, can provide a useful gauge of consumer spending. In many states, taxable sales also include construction materials, so some drilling down in the data is necessary to capture consumer spending, rather than consumer spending plus construction. In some states, however, the data are reported with such a long time lag that they are not useful.

KEY POINT

For regional companies, add to your dashboard the
measures of the industries that are important to
the region, as well as current employment data.

MANAGING IN THE REGIONAL BUSINESS CYCLE

The action steps for dealing with a regional downturn generally follow the pattern described in Chapter 7, but with additional considerations. The critical issue is whether the region is moving in the same direction as other regions. If this is the case, and the business cycle is affecting all areas of the country more or less equally, then ignore local considerations. However, if the region is different from the national economy or from other nearby regions, then there are additional threats and opportunities for the business leader.

For instance, consider a company selling services in a region that has entered a localized recession. The business has excess capacity. Selling additional services may have a very low marginal cost. It may be time to consider selling outside the company's traditional market. The lower-than-normal costs may justify the higher-than-normal marketing expenses that occur in new markets.

Similarly, a company that is primarily a producer in the local economy may get some great deals in a regional recession. This is the time to lock in long-term lease rates or buy the real estate that the business has been leasing. Local vendors may be willing to enter into long-term contracts at very

BUSINOMICS JARGON MADE CLEAR: *MARGINAL COST*

▶ "Marginal" is an economist's way of saying "for one additional unit." A company may estimate its average cost of production as total costs divided by the number of unit produced. However, that is not usually a good estimate of the cost of producing one additional unit. Much of the overhead and staff may already be on hand, to be paid whether production is increased or not. In such cases, the marginal cost is low. At other times, producing more goods will require additional capital expenditures and new hiring, as well as more raw materials, making marginal cost high.

favorable prices. Hiring topnotch employees becomes easier when local businesses are in distress.

Finally, corporate executives evaluating their regional managers need to take into account the condition of the regional economy, both in terms of the area's long-run trend as well as its short-term cycle. For example, suppose an Iowa banker grew her customer base by 2 percent in 2004, when the state's population was up less than half a percent and employment growth ran just a hair over 1 percent. She's growing market share. Let's say that her Arizona counterpart registered the same customer growth, 2 percent. Arizona's population grew by 3 percent in 2004, with an employment gain of over 3 percent. The Arizona banker is losing market share. One of these managers deserves a bonus, while the other needs a talking to, even though they both turned in identical customer growth rates.

KEY POINTS

The executive leading a regional company or division must know if his local conditions match conditions in the nation and other nearby regions.

Differences between the home region and other parts of the country create threats and opportunities, depending on whether the company is primarily selling or producing in the region.

BUSINOMICS

Industry Cycles:
Be Prepared for Trouble in
Your Sector of the Economy

WILLIAM B. CONERLY, PH.D.—As a college student in the early 1970s, I studied theoretical economics, but I also followed real businesses by reading *Forbes* magazine. I remember a disconnect between my academic studies of rational businesses and an article in *Forbes* about the paper industry. The article said that paper companies had once again overinvested in their plants, leading to overcapacity in the industry and a vicious price war. The writer asked if they would ever learn not to do that. I remember that article today, thirty-five years later, because events over the course of my career remind me of it regularly. The paper industry and other capital-intensive sectors have routinely experienced cycles of overinvestment and price weakness—and they never seem to learn.

All industries go through some cyclical fluctuation, as I described in Chapter 2. For the most part, there's nothing to be gained by thinking in terms of an industry cycle separate from the national cycle. For most industries, it's just the national cycle playing through the industry. However, capital-intensive sectors are different. They are still impacted by the national economy, but their own internal dynamics of capital investment drive huge swings in profitability.

WHY CAPITAL-INTENSIVE INDUSTRIES ARE DIFFERENT

Businesses that are capital-intensive behave differently than less capital-intensive firms. The most capital-intensive firms tend to have other characteristics that make them prone to cycles, including long lead times on expansions and slow rates of depreciation. In this section, we'll concentrate on industries that have all of these characteristics, ignoring the few exceptions.

A company will cover its costs, including an average risk-adjusted return on capital, in normal times. It will make extra profits at the top of the cycle, and either low profits or losses at the bottom of the cycle. In a recession, companies try to cut their expenses. No surprises here. However, the capital-intensive company finds that a large portion of its costs are capital costs. As such, they cannot easily be lowered.

In distress, a company will continue to operate a facility (a mine, a refinery, a factory, an airplane) when the revenue will exceed the variable costs associated with operating the facility. Variable costs are those costs that can be eliminated by cutting production, which may include labor costs, raw materials, and energy. Costs that are fixed in the short-run are overhead: interest and depreciation, insurance, and some administrative staff expense.

TABLE 10-A. Ten Most Capital-Intensive Industries

	Assets ($ billions)	Employment (thousands)	Assets/Employee ($/person)
Real estate	15,122	1.417	10,671.842
Oil and gas extraction	606	123	4,919,578
Pipeline transportation	102	39	2,615,979
Broadcasting and telecommunications	807	327	2,471,525
Utilities	1,308	570	2,294,633
Railroad transportation	285	224	1,272,200
Petroleum and coal products, refining	105	113	930,851
Water transportation	47	67	818,182
Mining, except oil and gas	101	207	486,721
Air transportation	248	515	480,963
TOTAL: **ALL PRIVATE SECTOR INDUSTRIES**	**27,043**	**109,862**	**246,152**

Let's look at a hypothetical example. The Conerly Coal Company in central Appalachia has the following cost structure:

TABLE 10-B. Conerly Coal

Variable costs (labor, energy)	$25 / ton
Fixed costs (overhead)	$20 / ton (based on average production)

Whenever the market price for our type of coal exceeds $25, we run the mine. If the price is only $26 per ton, we won't make enough to cover our overhead, but it is still worthwhile to operate. We make a $1 contribution to our overhead if we run the mine, but zero dollars toward overhead if we shut down.

The family also owns a (hypothetical) strawberry importing company. It has the following cost structure:

TABLE 10-C. Conerly Strawberries

Variable costs (labor, energy)	$40 / hundred pounds
Fixed costs (overhead)	$ 5 / hundred pounds (based on average production)

In both cases, a price of $45 covers our costs, based on average levels of production. The big difference is the mine's high capital costs, which entail high financing expense. In the coal company, we keep the mine running any time we can get at least $25 per ton. When demand is soft, we and all the other mines keep operating. No one likes it, but everyone keeps operating. The price has to fall sharply to induce enough demand to use up all of our production, so we're prone to large losses in bad times.

Most of the strawberry company's costs are variable. When times get bad and prices fall below $40, we lay off our workers and stop running our trucks. When the market for strawberries starts to weaken, companies in the industry close down, one by one. It's a smooth transition to a smaller industry.

This is the first distinction of capital-intensive industries: In bad times, they suffer large losses while continuing to operate. Prices plunge because so much of the industry's capacity is kept in production.

Note that this conclusion does not depend on demand for the product being more variable in one industry than another; it's strictly a result of the cost structure.

Companies vary from one another, even in the same industry. Some businesses will spend money for better equipment to lower their operating costs. The strawberry distributor, for example, might buy more fuel-efficient trucks. They have higher fixed costs (payments on the trucks) but lower variable costs (fuel for the trucks). Other competitors have higher variable costs but lower capital costs. There's been a mantra in business circles to drive production costs down. This is generally good, but sometimes the lesson is that those capital expenditures that bring down operating costs are good. That's a dangerous generalization. Sometimes they are good, no doubt, but capital expenditures limit flexibility. When a recession comes and production is cut, the capital costs are still being paid. The decision to spend money on equipment to reduce operating costs needs to be made carefully, with consideration of the loss of flexibility that results.

Now, let's consider another factor that accentuates cycles: long lead times for expansion. It takes years to get a coal mine ready for operation. Land acquisition, test drilling, planning, and development of mine-mouth infrastructure all add substantial time to the project. The same is true of producing oil and gas, building a fleet of airplanes, or laying track for a new railroad. It takes years, but when times are good, leaders in those industries build new capacity.

"In industries that are not so capital intensive, new capacity can be added quickly."

In industries that are not so capital intensive, such as our strawberry importing business, new capacity can be added quickly. A person with a Rolodex of industry contacts buys a used truck and he's in business. In less than a week he's moving berries. When pricing starts to look favorable, plenty of new competitors come out of the woodwork.

Back to coal. We add capacity when the market is strong, meaning that we *start* to add capacity when the market is strong. At that future date when the capacity will come on line, there's no telling what the market for the product will be like. However, it's unlikely to be strong. When the market is strong, prices move up, and everyone in the coal industry is minting money. There's no way for anyone to jump in quickly, so prices stay high for a couple of years. When one company is expanding, many other companies are also expanding. The unfortunate result is that many companies bring their new mining capacity on line at the same time. Even if the macro economy is still strong, the large increase in capacity will bring prices down. Furthermore, remember the cost structure: once a mine has the capacity, it operates it. That goes for all of the companies in this stupid industry. Profits take a dive, and some of the companies have to file bankruptcy.

The strawberry business isn't like this. When the market improves, a few people enter quickly, while existing businesses expand. It happens with little delay. Those who take a month or two to think about their decision find that the market has softened because of the new capacity. The industry does not tend to overshoot its needs, at least not substantially.

Now let's add the final blow to capital-intensive industries: slow rates of depreciation. The capacity that's been added in coal mining does not wear out quickly, and it does not become obsolete very fast. When there is excess capacity, it sticks around. That's generally true of capital-intensive industries, but there are notable exceptions, such as semi-conductor manufacturing.

In summary, we have discussed three elements that combine to make capital-intensive industries very prone to cycles of overbuilding:

- Capital intensity itself
- Long lead times to put new capacity in place
- Low rates of depreciation

The result of these three elements is an industry prone to severe swings of overcapacity and undercapacity. Pricing swings in the opposite direction, with huge profits when the industry has underestimated its future need for capacity and large losses when too much capacity is in place.

The time required to work off the excess capacity varies from industry to industry. The fastest times are recorded by industries with fast trend growth of demand and fast depreciation rates. In these sectors, demand growth absorbs excess capacity, and depreciation reduces the amount of effective capital. Depreciation in this sense is economic depreciation, which is seldom the same as tax or accounting depreciation. Economic depreciation considers both physical wearing out of equipment as well as obsolescence. For semiconductor fabrication plants, the machinery seldom wears out. It simply becomes obsolete before wear-and-tear causes problems. In this industry, excess capacity is quickly reduced.

Chart 10.1 on the following page shows the process for a slow-growth industry. We assume that the underlying trend growth rate of demand is 1 percent per year, but that actual demand has a cyclical pattern above and below the trend.

We have depreciation at 3 percent per year, and additional capacity added whenever demand reaches 90 percent of capacity, in increments equal to 10 percent of capacity.

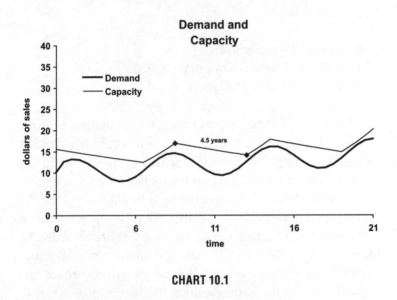

CHART 10.1

In Chart 10.1, shown here, we note the time required to work off excess capacity, 4.5 years. Some of the working off happened through depreciation, as shown by the downward-sloping parts of the capacity line. In addition, the cyclical recovery of demand, combined with the 1 percent trend growth of demand, eventually necessitates addition of more capacity.

Chart 10.2, on the next page, shows the same industry assumptions, except that demand grows more rapidly, 3 percent in this case rather than 1 percent previously.

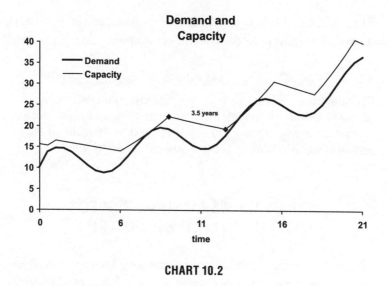

CHART 10.2

The time to work off excess capital is about one year shorter. The strong trend growth helps reduce excess capacity in short order.

The difference caused by the industry's underlying growth trend and depreciation rate must be kept in mind. In high-tech, overcapacity can occur, but it typically works itself out in short order. Slow-growing industries include pipelines and utilities, where not only is underlying demand growth slow, but depreciation is glacial.

An industry cycle due to overcapacity can occur without an overall economic downturn or recession. However, an economic downturn, with falling demand for the products of capital-intensive industries, will hasten or aggravate a cycle. An industry that might have had moderate capacity will find that it has excess capacity in a recession. Then high fixed costs and low depreciation rates damage the industry disproportionately to the overall economic cycle.

Capital-intensive industries are prone to cycles of overinvestment in capacity, leading to prolonged periods of unprofitable operations.

Cycles in capital-intensive industries are worsened by long lead times for capacity additions and low rates of depreciation.

THE EARLY WARNING SYSTEM FOR CAPITAL-INTENSIVE INDUSTRIES

The extra elements that a capital-intensive business needs in its early warning system are straightforward: ways to measure new capacity coming on line in its industry. An actual timeline is possible. For example, the creation of downtown office space is usually announced and reported in the news. Listing estimated completion dates and floor area allows competitors to see the region's total available space both now and in the coming years. Similarly, aircraft orders are announced in the press, allowing airlines to estimate how many planes their competitors will put into service in the coming years.

More often, estimates of new capital spending are available from industry sources. Experienced observers can see the beginnings of overinvestment, so long as they are not caught up in the current euphoria of favorable prices and the optimism of ever-growing prices.

A capital-intensive company's early warning system must include indicators of new capacity being added in the industry.

MANAGING THROUGH THE INDUSTRY CYCLE

Managers in capital-intensive industries need to recognize their industry's capital intensity. This sounds obvious, but recognition will influence a wide variety of business decisions. The capital-intensive industry is prone to wide swings in profitability, making awareness of the industry cycle critical.

Next, business leaders should understand typical lengths of expansions in their industries. As with the economy, no industry goes through cycles of a regular, periodic nature. However, the manager should understand the patterns of the past business cycles. In Chapter 5, we saw how to compute the average length of a recession for industry data. In the capital-intensive industry, it is more important to know the average length of an expansion. When business picks up and profitability starts to improve, there will be a temptation to add capacity. That is fine if the expansion will continue for enough years that the new capacity will be on line for at least a couple of years of the boom. However, if an expansion is only going to last three years, and if a capital addition will require two years to design and build, then the project will only contribute to earnings for one year. Then the weak pricing cycle will set in, and the business leader will wish that he had not added the new capacity at all. In short, it's good practice to invest in new capacity early in an expansion that is likely to last for several years longer than the capacity addition time lag.

As the cycle progresses, prices will rise and competitors will announce new expansion plans. This is the time to stop adding new capacity. Enjoy the strong profits, sock away the cash, and wait for the industry's overexpansion to play out.

This is hard to do, as it flies in the face of what one's competitors are doing. Think contrarian.

When the industry's new capacity additions are completed, and new capacity is now available to meet customer demand, product prices will fall. Formerly profitable companies will find that they are not able to recover all of their costs, especially if they borrowed heavily to finance the new expansions. Now it is time for some bottom fishing. Having accumulated a supply of cash in the boom, the wise leader looks to pick up new capacity when it is cheap. Once again, the strategy is contrarian. Doom and gloom will pervade industry conferences and trade journals. The overhang of productive capacity will dampen spirits as well as profitability. Pundits will proclaim the end of the industry. There is always a mixture of news about any industry, and at the bottom of the market writers will gather up all the bad news into one pessimistic package. This is the signal to buy.

The temptation to avoid is to move too quickly. The astute business leader avoided the excesses of the boom, paid down debt, and amassed a horde of cash. The business is well poised to acquire a weak company. This is so much fun that everyone on the team is anxious to get going. Be patient. Bide your time. Wait for real distress. Monitor the financial condition of weak competitors. If they are publicly traded, know their financials in detail. If they are privately held, seek information from industry sources, such as vendors, about their condition, especially whether they are able to make payments on a timely basis.

When a good opportunity presents itself, buy good productive capacity at a significant discount to the cost of new construction. Industry cycles almost invariably turn themselves around, and the company will be well poised for the next expansion. Buying early, before the capacity is needed, is entirely appropriate if the capacity is inexpensive. This strategy significantly outperforms the run-with-the-herd approach of adding on capacity when the market is booming.

KEY POINTS		
Recognize and understand the nature of cycles in your industry.	In boom times, don't add capacity. Instead, amass cash.	During industry downturns, buy out weak competitors' capacity.

SUMMING UP

Capital-intensive businesses face additional problems that other companies don't face. They are vulnerable to profit-killing cycles of overbuilding, and they thus need an addition to their early warning system that monitors industry-level capital investment.

Economics and the Stock Market

WILLIAM B. CONERLY, PH.D.—Does the economy move the stock market? Does the stock market move the economy? In this chapter, we continue our ongoing look at the economy from the business leader's perspective, but we also consider the economy from the investor's perspective.

The first rule is to recognize that the economy and the stock market do not move in lockstep.

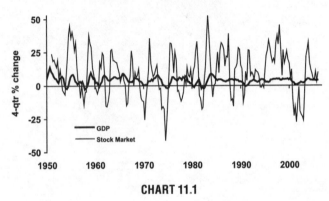

The Stock Market & GDP

CHART 11.1

The stock market is much more volatile than the economy. Economic output never grows by much more than 10 percent in a four-quarter period, nor does it decline by more than 3 percent. Yet the stock market has seen changes as high as up 53 percent and down 41 percent.

However, there is some connection if one looks closely. The times when the stock market was declining were usually times when the economy was soft; the economy was not necessarily in recession, but it was at least decelerating. The economy weakened in 2000 and 2001, while the stock market tanked.

The bear market of 1974 illustrates the key points, as shown in Chart 11.2. To better see the relationship between the two series, they have been plotted on different scales (see the following page).

First, notice that in early 1973, the stock market began to decelerate, even while the economy continued to accelerate. The swing in stock prices happened before the change in economic growth rate.

Second, the stock market turned positive (went above the zero axis) while the economy was still declining. Stocks continued to grow rapidly in advance of economic growth, until mid-1975. In other words, stocks were a leading indicator. One could have forecast the economy by watching changes in stock prices.

refer to the following page

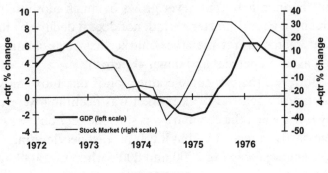

CHART 11.2

There are exceptions, such as in 1977, when the economy enjoyed strong gains of about 5 percent but stock prices dropped by over 17 percent.

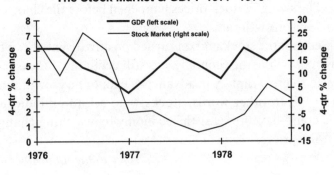

CHART 11.3

THE ECONOMY'S IMPACT ON THE STOCK MARKET

Stock market prices incorporate expectations about the future course of corporate earnings, as well as the interest rate at which investors discount future earnings. Both of these factors should be affected by the state of the economy. We saw in Chapter 2 that corporate profits rise and fall with the economy, but with exaggerated movement. When investors expect future corporate profits to be weak, it's often because of expectations of a weak economy. A simple model of stock prices has today's price being the sum of future earnings, with each year's earning being discounted to a present value. When the interest rate used to discount future earnings is high, then the present value of those earnings is low. Thus, high interest rates by themselves would depress the stock market, even if high interest rates had no impact on the economy. In short, there's good reason to expect stock market prices to reflect the investment community's beliefs about current and future conditions. The connection between the 1929 stock market crash and the Great Depression is far more than coincidence.

BUSINOMICS JARGON MADE CLEAR: *PRESENT VALUE*

▶ "Present value" has a very specific definition to economists. Behind the definition is the truism that we would rather have a dollar today than a dollar a year from today. But if given a choice, we might say that ninety-four cents today is about equal to $1 a year from today. If that's what we think, then ninety-four cents is the present value of $1 a year from today. The math is $0.94 = 1.00 / (1 + r)$, where "*r*" denotes the interest rate. In this case, *r* is about 6 percent. More commonly, the interest rate is first determined, then the present value is calculated using the formula.

Just because the stock market reflects investors' expectations for the economy does not mean that the market will be correlated with actual economic events. It is possible that investors forecast the economy so poorly that stock prices move independently of actual changes in the economy. It's possible, but that's not what actually happens. Investors are moderately capable of forecasting the economy, which leads to stock prices that reflect moderately well what the economy actually does in the future. The stock market isn't a perfect forecaster of future economic activity, but it's better than throwing darts.

One argument against using the stock market as a guide to future economic activity is the well-known excesses to which the market is prone. We noted above that the market has gained or lost more than 40 percent in one year's time. However, the economy has never quite justified such a large swing in valuation. Even those of us who are inclined to believe that financial markets are pretty efficient must admit that sometimes investors seem to be swept up in their emotions.

In a nutshell, the connection between the economy and the stock market runs something like this: The economy affects expected profits and interest rates, both of which in turn affect the stock market.

The formation of expectations is imperfect, and thus the linkage between the economy and the stock market is imperfect.

KEY POINT

The economy affects the stock market through current
interest rates and expectations for future profits.

THE STOCK MARKET AS A LEADING INDICATOR OF THE ECONOMY

If investors are doing a good job of evaluating stock prices, then the stock market will be a leading indicator of economic activity. A business leader who is trying to anticipate swings in sales volume would be able to use the stock market as an indicator of future changes.

In fact, the stock market is a leading indicator of the economy. Major swings in the stock market have, in fact, anticipated major swings in the economy. However, this relationship is not perfect. Paul Samuelson, the Nobel laureate in economics from MIT, famously said that the stock market has forecast nine of the last five recessions. The example of 1977, charted above, illustrates Samuelson's point.

However, statistical analysis of all the data available indicates that stock market prices do help forecast the economy, but they are far from definitive. As a result, a business leader might put stock market prices on the early warning system. In this usage, stock prices are simply a way to look at investors' forecasts of the economy. However, we prefer to look directly at forecasts of the economy. It's possible that stock prices are down because investors anticipate falling price-earnings ratios, rather than falling earnings. In this instance, the stock market does not provide good information about market expectations for the economy. As a business leader, you would be better served looking at consensus forecasts, as described in Chapter 6.

KEY POINT

The stock market tends to move before the economy, but it does not, by itself, do a good job of forecasting the economy.

THE STOCK MARKET'S IMPACT ON THE ECONOMY

So far there is evidence that the economy affects the stock market. Could causation run in the other direction; that is, could the stock market affect the economy? Schoolchildren learn that the Great Depression followed the stock market crash of 1929. Could stock prices cause changes in economic activity?

The logic behind this assertion typically begins with capital spending. Business capital spending is a small portion of GDP (about 10 percent), but it is quite volatile. James Tobin, the Nobel laureate from Yale University, developed a simple ratio that he called "q," which everyone else calls "Tobin's q." Tobin begins with the stock market's value of a company. Then he looks at the replacement cost of the company's assets. Tobin's q is the ratio of the stock market value to the replacement value of the assets. Tobin hypothesized that companies would invest in physical capital when q was greater than 1. Suppose that a company has a q of 1.5. Then adding \$1 of physical assets would boost its stock price by \$1.50, which sounds like a pretty good buy.

When the stock market is strong, many companies will have a q of more than 1 and will thus be investing in physical capital, stimulating business capital spending. When the stock market is weak, the q for many companies will fall below 1, and they'll stop adding new capital. The stock market can thus influence business capital spending, and therefore the overall economy.

Companies that want to expand their physical capital when their q is low may buy other companies. T. Boone Pickens, the oilman and corporate raider, remarked once when the stock market was low that it was cheaper to drill for oil on Wall Street. As a result, the contrarians who are looking to buy when the outlook is dismal do not stimulate demand for new capital goods, they merely bid up the price of existing assets.

Even if corporate executives are not consciously weighing stock values against asset costs, they may be acting as if they do. Corporate issuance of stock rises when the stock market is strong, enabling companies to fund the expansions that they already wanted to do. On the downside, weak stock prices reduce a company's willingness to issue new shares, limiting the business's discretionary spending.

The tech boom of the late 1990s seemed to validate Tobin's model. Investors were offering wild valuations to any two computer geeks with an idea for an Internet company. As a result, every geek with a friend sought out venture capital and went ahead and started a company. In short, if the stock market will place a high valuation on something, people will provide it.

By itself, however, Tobin's q does a mediocre job of explaining capital spending. It fits the data well for the 1950s and 1960s, misses the mark for the 1970s and 1980s, and then looks good once again in the 1990s. Also note that capital spending is just one part of the economy, and it's possible for other sectors to make up for weakness in capital spending.

My conclusion is that in extreme cases, the stock market can have an effect on the economy, but most commonly stock market changes are the result of economic fluctuations.

KEY POINT

Swings in stock prices can cause swings in capital spending, which can, in turn, affect the overall economy. The effects on aggregate output, though, tend to be small.

AN INVESTOR'S PERSPECTIVE ON THE ECONOMY

Investors have different perspectives from business executives and owners (though business executives and owners are often investors). At times when the economy was strong, I've heard people complain vociferously about economic conditions. Upon probing, it turns out that they assumed the economy was lousy if their stocks were not recording double-digit returns. Lesson number one, then, is that the economy is not the same thing as the stock market.

People who are focused on their investments usually don't care if GDP is up or down, so long as their stocks are up. So let's take an investor's perspective on the economy. Current stock market expectations embody the market's view of the outlook for profits and interest rates. By "market's view," we mean that the aggregation of all the opinions of all the investors in the market results in a price for each stock. For instance, the market may base prices on 4 percent growth in GDP next year. Are stocks a good buy then? Four percent is above-average GDP growth, so one might be tempted to invest more heavily. However, if that 4 percent growth of GDP actually occurs, investors will *not* earn extraordinary profits, because the 4 percent growth was already embodied in the market. What will change the market is growth coming in higher or lower than expected.

The investor looking at the economy should ask if the consensus forecast is wrong, and if so, how is it wrong? The investor who believes the consensus economic forecast cannot beat the market with that forecast because he believes in the market forecast. That investor would be better off studying specific stocks rather than trying to guess the entire market.

The consensus forecast consists of a lot more than **GDP**, though. The market forecast includes the outlook for every sector of the economy. The investor can review components of the consensus forecast to find out where he thinks it's wrong. If, for example, the investor thinks that consumer spending will be stronger than the consensus forecast, then it's time to buy stocks in companies that benefit from discretionary consumer spending, such as automobiles, home electronics, furniture, and so on. The investor who thinks the outlook for capital spending is not as strong as the consensus view should sell stocks in heavy equipment manufacturers. The key issue here is not whether the investor thinks capital spending will increase, but whether the investor's forecast is higher or lower than the consensus. If everyone else is wildly optimistic about a sector, then the investor who is only moderately optimistic should act like a pessimist and sell stocks in that sector. In relative terms, that investor is a pessimist.

For example, in January of 2005, the consensus of forecasters was that long-term interest rates would rise throughout the year, by almost a full percentage point. An investor who believed that rates would *not* rise, or that they would rise at a slower rate, could play that forecast by buying stock in home-building companies, which are strongly affected by mortgage rates. In fact, long rates rose by only a quarter of a percentage point, and homebuilding benefited from the benign mortgage rate environment, rising 15 percent through the year. In comparison, the Standard & Poor's 500 gained only 3 percent. In this case, a prescient forecaster would have anticipated some increase in mortgage rates. But because this increase was less than the consensus, the prescient forecaster made a bullish bet on homebuilding.

Investors looking for an easy way to make money should be cautious about this approach. (Indeed, they should be cautious about most any approach.) The ability to out-predict the consensus is rare. Careful analyses of forecast accuracy over time have generally shown that the consensus—the average of the forecasts—is more accurate than the most accurate individual forecaster. So an investor may beat the consensus one year, but it is very unlikely that the investor can continue to beat the consensus year after year.

KEY POINT

Investors should gauge their economic expectations against the market consensus, rather than in absolute terms.

MANAGING THROUGH THE STOCK MARKET CYCLE

The key issue for most corporations watching the stock market is when to sell stock and when to buy their stock back. Our advice is straightforward: Buy low, sell high.

The challenge facing the financial executive is knowing when the stock price is high or low. Most CEOs and CFOs who have spoken to me on the subject believed that the stock market undervalued their company's stock. Sometimes that's true—and sometimes it's not. Executives tend to have a huge financial—and ego—investment when it comes to the value of their company's stock. Compounding the challenge is that they may not feel comfortable buying low or selling high. For instance, let's say that XYZ Corporation's stock is considered overvalued by the company management. Looking forward, they see only weak growth prospects. The simple answer is to sell the stock. For the corporation, that means issuing more shares in exchange for cash. But what is this company going to do with the cash? Its growth prospects are already weak, at least in the minds of senior management. It probably does not need the cash and cannot deploy it at a high return. Issuing equity in exchange for cash, then investing the cash in treasury bills, sounds like a losing strategy.

Follow the plan more closely, though. Assume that the stock price eventually declines to where management expected it to be. It uses the proceeds from the earlier stock issuance to buy back shares at a significant discount to the price at which it had issued the shares. In other words, it first sold high, then it bought back low. The number of shares outstanding ends up equal to the number that was outstanding in the beginning, but the company has extra cash in the treasury. That's a winning strategy.

Another way to play the overvalued company position is to simply sell the business as a whole. Note that we are discussing what makes sense for the shareholders, not what fits with the goals and aspirations of the men and women running the company.

The more common case is one in which the company thinks that its stock is undervalued and that the company has great prospects ahead. When stock is low, then buy it back. However, in this instance, the company may feel that buying back its stock will leave it with insufficient cash to implement its great plans. Let's assume that in this case, the corporation's management has carefully removed all hubris from its estimate of its stock price. (A big assumption, but let's make it for the sake of the example.) The best course of action, if possible, is to borrow money in order to fund both the stock buyback and the expansion plans. However, if borrowing constraints limit debt finance, then the company has to estimate the potential return from its stock price rising to projected levels, compared to the return from the new capital spending. This is a simple ROI (return on investment) calculation. If the company's stock is at $20, but management thinks that a fair value is $30, then it's looking at a 50 percent return from a stock buyback. Unless the company is looking at blockbuster technology, it's rare to get a 50 percent return on investment over a time span of a year or two.

KEY POINT

Corporate executives should buy back stock when they believe that their stock price is unusually low, and issue new shares when their stock price appears to be overvalued.

The Economic Case for America

WILLIAM B. CONERLY, PH.D.—An entrepreneur wanted to talk to me about a doom-and-gloom economics book he had just read. This was back in the late 1980s, when I was the economist for a major bank. The entrepreneur, whom we'll call Mr. Smith to protect the mistaken, had been a good customer of the bank, and we were looking forward to financing his expansion from two facilities to four. But then he read the awful book and expressed doubts to his loan officer. The banker called me in to try to save the deal.

We toured his business before sitting down to lunch. In the tour it became obvious that Smith really knew his customers and their needs, and he had a strong drive to serve them. He had several competitors, but he had built a pricing structure for bundled products and services that fit the needs of a significant segment of his market. His pricing structure, his understanding of his customers' needs, and his drive to deliver outstanding service ensured the success of his company.

The book that he had read forecast a major depression for the economy that would strike in 1990. "The depression of the 1990s is likely to be the worst in history," the author wrote. The depression would be so severe that stocks would collapse, banks would fail, and readers should withdraw money from banks and bury the currency in their back yards. There was a mild recession, which began in July 1990 and was over by March 1991. It was not severe, not even close to the worst in history, and it lasted less than one year, not the seven years predicted in the book.

I was unable to convince Mr. Smith that the economy would continue to grow, and he decided not to expand his business. Now I drive past operations run by his competitors, who have taken market share from this talented business leader. He was excellent at building a business, but he was terribly mistaken to bet against the continued success of the American economy.

The U.S. economy has a long track record of strong growth. Certainly there have been recessions, and even a long depression, but the most dominant fact about historical performance of the U.S. economy is the persistence of its growth. Growth is not something that happens just once in a while; it is a typical feature of the economic landscape. The Great Depression showed up in the 1930s, with the subsequent recovery getting the economy back on track. Recessions are bumps in the road, not catastrophes—though it's always easier to say that the recession wasn't so bad when it wasn't your job that was lost.

Much of this book has dealt with recessions: how to anticipate them, how to prepare for them, how to take advantage of them. Despite this preoccupation with the macabre side of economics, I'm really quite optimistic. Yes, recessions *will* happen. But a severe depression is very unlikely.

Recessions will come and go. Some of them may be as severe as the sharp decline of the early 1980s, or possibly worse. The likelihood of a major down cycle, comparable to the Great Depression, is very low. Planning for the garden-variety recessions described in this book strikes a reasonable balance between being ready for both growth and recession. Planning for another depression requires companies to abandon most growth opportunities, and that is too pessimistic for their own good. As a business manager, you should plan for future cycles in the range of post–World War II recessions.

CONTINUED GROWTH IN THE LONG TERM

The basic view of long-term growth used here is that goods and services are produced with capital and labor. Capital consists of the tools used to manufacture products and to provide services. Simply put, the more capital a country has, the higher its potential output. The level of output produced from a given quantity of labor and capital is determined by current technology.

Labor is all kinds of effort that people make, both the sweat-of-the-brow variety and the stare-out-the-window kind of work in which I specialize. More labor also translates into more output.

Businesses in the United States have been increasing their capital stock almost continuously for a couple of centuries. Some of the equipment has worn out, some has become obsolete, but they keep adding new capital in substantial amounts. Betting against growth pretty much requires a bet against further increases in capital.

Labor, the second element in the traditional view of economic growth, complements capital. The U.S. population continues to grow in two ways. "Natural increase" in population is simply the difference between the number of births and burials in a year. The second component of growth is net migration, or the number of people moving in minus the number moving out.

Birth rates are certainly declining, and that implies natural increase in population diminishing toward zero over time. Immigration, though, is limited only by political concerns about the speed with which our country can absorb newcomers and about the value that they yield to the country as a whole. Despite periodic controversies about how many immigrants to accept, and about what to do with illegal immigrants, it seems reasonable to forecast a continuing inflow of new residents coming to America from poorer countries.

The labor supply is about more than the sheer number of people, though. It's also a matter of how many of the people living in the country are actually at work. That depends, in turn, on two issues: how many people want to work, and how many of them actually find work.

The United States ranks high in the percentage of its population that is either working or looking for work, the "labor force participation rate." Our high rate is in line with other high-income countries and well above slower-growing countries such as Italy and Spain.

The United States also performs well at getting jobs for people who want to work. Our unemployment rate compares very favorably with developed European countries, largely because of our more flexible labor markets. By "flexible," economists mean that the labor markets adapt to changing circumstances. For example, many European countries have job security laws that make it very expensive for companies to fire workers. Those laws also make companies very hesitant to hire in the first place. In contrast, American companies are relatively quick to hire, knowing that they can lay off the work force if necessary. While this practice may appear harsher than that of the European countries, it actually results in greater job creation, helping people who want to work.

The primary labor market challenge that businesses will face in the coming decades is the retirement of the baby boom generation. We will have a decade with growth in demand for goods and services, but little growth in the labor supply. Companies will face higher wage costs, and outsourcing will become even more common. This should not threaten the economy overall, but it will require businesses to find new ways to meet their human resource needs. The result of immigration and our flexible labor markets will be continued growth of the labor supply, although the decade of the 2010s will be a challenge due to the demographic cycle.

> "The primary labor market challenge that businesses will face in the coming decades is the retirement of the baby boom generation."

With regard to capital and labor, businesses will continue to sink new investments in this country, and ambitious foreigners will continue to want to move here. These assumptions are fundamental underpinnings of my conclusion that the U.S. economy will continue to grow.

Despite America's imperfections, as a forecaster I'm highly confident that we will continue to be a place where businesses invest capital and to which people from around the world flock by the thousands. The macroeconomic implication of this is that businesses here should count on long-term growth continuing.

IDEAS WILL MAKE US GROW

The basic approach used in modern economics to study long-term growth has been based on the "tools and people" model, with extensive mathematical elaboration. A side trend to discuss the importance of property rights and enforcement of contract has recently developed. In the last two decades, though, a new way of looking at long run growth has been presented under the title "the New Growth Theory."

Suppose that you have a dollar, and I have a dollar. If I give you my dollar, and you give me your dollar, then we each have a dollar again. But suppose that I have an idea, and you have an idea, and then we swap. Afterwards, we each have two ideas.

This insight is crucial to the long-term outlook. The New Growth Theory emphasizes the importance of ideas. Ideas include scientific knowledge of all kinds. Ideas include engineering knowledge, such as described by patents. Ideas also include craftsmanship of a wide variety. When a mechanic knows just how much force to apply to a bolt to tighten it, without overtightening it, he is applying an idea.

Ideas are at least as important as the equipment and buildings used by businesses. And ideas have a really cool trait: multiple people can use them at one time. That's not generally true of other stuff. A cash register can only be used by one cashier at a time. To have two cashiers working, the store needs two cash registers. But once someone has the idea to display *People* magazine next to the cash register, that idea can be replicated endlessly.

This insight into ideas has stunning implications for growth. It means that so long as the ideas flow, growth will continue. In the modern United States, we are open to international visits and commerce. Our companies invest overseas, and foreign companies invest in the United States. Americans subscribe to the *Economist* magazine from London, just as Japanese businessmen read *Fortune*. American companies have borrowed Japanese techniques for making cars. Southeast Asian factories have borrowed American techniques for making electronics. And we will soon take advantage of new Chinese ideas. As China develops, more and more of their first-rate minds will be developing ideas that everyone in the world can use. Unleashing that creative energy will give the entire world a huge boost. Add in the growth of India and other countries, and the flow of new ideas will be staggeringly huge in the coming decades.

So long as our borders and news media—and the Internet—are open, then ideas will flow freely, stimulating further growth in productivity.

SUMMING IT ALL UP

Despite the evidence that the U.S. economy will continue to grow over the next few decades, and probably longer, one hears pessimistic skeptics regularly. For economists and futurists, there's a lure to the doom-and-gloom approach: It sells books. Consider, for example, the book described at the beginning of this chapter, Ravi Batra's *The Great Depression of 1990*, which was on the *New York Times* bestseller list for fifty-two weeks. Batra's recommendation for people with wealth was to sell their stocks. Bank accounts should be closed, he advised, and currency saved, presumably stuffed in a mattress or the buried in the back yard.

What would have come from following Batra's advice? If you read the book when it was first published in August 1985, and implemented his plan in December of that year, by the end of 1992 your cash would have lost 38 percent of its purchasing power due to inflation. (Batra predicted deflation rather than inflation, using a 25 percent decline in prices in one of his examples.) What if you had, instead, invested your money in the stock market? Despite the bear market of 1991, your investments would have exceeded inflation by 61 percent. Even if you had switched to the safest investment vehicle around, treasury bills, you would have only lost 6 percent to inflation. The only people who made money from Batra's book were Batra and his publisher.

When push comes to shove, the business leader must make a decision whether to commit money to the enterprise or not. The wisdom of that decision will only be known over time. It depends on many factors specific to the business, such as the market for its product and its cost of producing the product. Those factors, in turn, are partially dependent on the overall growth of the economy. The economy won't bail anyone out of truly stupid mistakes, but it can provide an environment in which moderately good decisions lead to profitability.

For my money, I'm betting that the U.S. economy will continue to grow. I'd peg population growth a little slower than in recent decades, and I'd put productivity growth a bit higher than in the past two decades. Roll it all together, and we'll have about the same growth rate, in the long run, as we've had in the recent past. Recessions will come and go. Overall, you can bet on the total volume of economic activity to continue to grow in this country.

Data Sources

SIC/NAICS Classifications

Many data series are classified by NAICS code, which is the successor to the SIC code. All types of businesses fall into a particular classification. Groups of similar classifications share the first few digits of their numbers. For example, the six-digit NAICS code 336612 represents "Boat Building." The four-digit code 3366 represents "Ship and Boat Building." The three-digit code 336 represents "Transportation Equipment Manufacturing."

A link to the entire list of codes, with descriptions, appears on the Resources page of *www.businomics.com*.

National Income and Product Accounts

The other classification system that's useful is the National Income and Product Accounts (NIPA). These accounts add up the various components of gross domestic product. The major NIPA categories, as described in Chapter 1, are the following:

Gross Domestic Product
Personal Consumption Expenditures
- Durable goods
- Nondurable goods
- Services

Gross Private Domestic Investment
- Fixed investment
- Nonresidential
- Structures

- Equipment and software
- Residential
- Change in private inventories

Net Exports of Goods and Services
- Exports
  1. Goods
  2. Services
- Imports
  1. Goods
  2. Services

Government Consumption Expenditures and Gross Investment
- Federal
  1. National defense
  2. Nondefense
- State and local

The U.S. Bureau of Economic Analysis provides figures for spending in each of these categories, with substantial detail within the categories. For instance, consumer spending on durable goods is divided into categories, one of which is "Video and audio goods, including musical instruments and computer goods." This category gives an idea of the level of detail that is available in the government statistics.

Government Agencies

After finding an industry's classification by both NAICS and NIPA, it's time to go looking for data. Different government agencies collect statistics. This section describes the major sources, but many other specialized government agencies also provide data. For example, the Department of Agriculture makes available statistics on production and prices for different crops. The Department of Energy produces voluminous statistics, published by the Energy Information Administration.

The following listing shows the major data sources that cover many different industries. Current links to their Web sites appear on the Resources page of *www.businomics.com.*

National Income and Product Accounts: U.S. Bureau of Economic Analysis. In addition to the quarterly GDP accounts, also look at the monthly consumer income and expenditures data in the "personal income" reports.

Consumer Spending

Retail sales: U.S. Census Bureau. The retail sales data are organized by type of store. Furniture store sales, for example, cover the entire volume of sales of stores that primarily sell furniture. The category does not include sales of furniture at department stores or office supply stores. The information is most useful, therefore, to companies selling in typical stores. Executives at businesses that manufacture products will find some value here, but they must keep in mind the limitations of the data.

Specific types of consumer spending information are also published by the departments of agriculture, energy, health and human services, housing, and transportation.

Business Investment

Business spending on equipment can be tracked by the manufacturing data published by the Census Bureau. These data are broken down by types of products, as well as by four-digit NAICS codes. The report shows figures on orders for new equipment as well as shipments, which correspond to sales. To track aggregate spending on business equipment, the Census Bureau publishes nondefense capital spending. Many analysts also strip out transportation equipment, because aircraft orders are very large and change substantially from month to month.

Business spending on structures is reported by the Census Bureau in their measures of "construction put in place." These statistics report dollars as they are spent. A large project that will take two years to complete shows up over the two years of construction, not just when the building is finished. McGraw-Hill also publishes useful statistics on construction through their F.W. Dodge subsidiary. These figures are available on a subscription basis.

Residential Construction

The primary sources of information on residential construction come from the Census Bureau's monthly report on housing starts and permits. Unlike most data, these are available for individual states.

Inventories

Inventory changes are a part of the national income and products accounts because it's necessary to add this to sales in order to measure production. However, most businesses are not interested in the aggregate inventories in the economy. Figures on inventories of specific products are useful and are usually found in industry-specific databases.

Government Spending

Businesses selling to the government can monitor spending trends through projected budgets. Federal projections are available from the Office of Management and Budget. Most states and municipalities also publish their budget information, but businesses selling to numerous jurisdictions need a picture of aggregate state and local government spending. The Census Bureau collects such information but with a substantial time lag. The Rockefeller Institute of Government has substantial information on the subject.

Exports
Voluminous data on exports and imports is published by the Census Bureau.

Regional Data Sources and Calculations
Employment data are available from the U.S. Bureau of Labor Statistics. Every state has a state labor market information service that works in conjunction with the BLS. Generally, the state employment service will post new data before the BLS. The data formats vary from state to state, sometimes making manipulation of the data harder, and sometimes easier. Check out both your state's data agency as well as the BLS. Web addresses are available at *www .businomics.com*.

Data on earnings by region and industry are available from the U.S. Bureau of Economic Analysis. Again, there is a link to their Web site from *www.businomics.com*.

Calculating a Regional Similarity Index
For both the United States and the state being studied, download data about the personal income category "total earnings," which includes a breakdown by industry. For the United States, calculate each industry's share of total earnings. Now do the same for the state: Calculate each industry's share of earnings within the state. The next step is to take the absolute value of the difference between the percentage

of earnings in the state and the percentage of earnings in the United States. Make this calculation for each industry. Sum up all of the differences, and subtract from one. This is your similarity index.

Calculating a Location Quotient

The ingredients for the calculation are data on earnings by sector. The data are available from the U.S. Bureau of Economic Analysis (see *www.businomics.com* for the current Web address). From the BEA, download data on earnings by industry.

The columns on your spreadsheet should look like the headings of Table 9-C, on page 206 in Chapter 9. However, you'll have data on every industry, not just farm earnings. Here's a quick guide to how I set up the columns:

Column	Title	Entries
A.	Label	with the BEA data
B.	U.S.	Data from BEA
C.	% of total	For each inquiry, divide U.S. industry earnings in dollars by total U.S. "Earnings by Place of Work"
D.	Your state data from BEA	
E.	% of total	For each industry, divide state industry earnings in dollars by total state "Earnings by Place of Work"
F.	Location Quotient	Column E divided by Column C
G.	$ difference	State earnings in the industry, minus the following: state Earnings by Place of Work, multiplied by U.S. % of total for that industry.

This is a good use of Excel's conditional formatting feature, which allows you to make bold the entries that are relatively large. Click Format, then Conditional Formatting.

INDEX

ABOUT THE AUTHOR

DR. BILL CONERLY is the principal of Conerly Consulting, LLC, which helps business leaders make more profitable decisions through a better understanding of the economy. He holds a Ph.D. in economics from Duke University and an undergraduate economics degree from New College.

He worked in corporate economics positions at Pacific Gas and Electric Company, NERCO Inc., and at First Interstate Bank, where he was senior vice president.

Dr. Conerly is coauthor of *Thinking Economics*, a high school textbook used in twenty-four states. Two of his articles are required reading in graduate courses at MIT and Wharton. He has been quoted in *Fortune* magazine, the *Wall Street Journal*, and *USA Today*, and interviewed on *The News Hour with Jim Lehrer*, CNN, and CNBC.

Dr. Conerly is chairman of the board of Cascade Policy Institute, a member of the Governor's Council of Economic Advisors, and a Senior Fellow at the National Center for Policy Analysis.

He lives in Lake Oswego, Oregon, with his wife, Christina West, and his sons, Peter and Tom Conerly. In his free time, he races sailboats.

More information about the author is available at *www .businomics.com*.